Legislating for Harmony
Partnership Under the
Children Act 1989

Legislating for Harmony
Partnership Under the Children Act 1989

edited by
Felicity Kaganas, Michael King and Christine Piper

Jessica Kingsley Publishers
London and Bristol, Pennsylvania

First published in the United Kingdom in 1995 by
Jessica Kingsley Publishers Ltd
116 Pentonville Road
London N1 9JB, England
and
1900 Frost Road, Suite 101
Bristol, PA 19007, USA

Copyright © 1995 Felicity Kaganas, Michael King and
Christine Piper

Library of Congress Cataloging in Publication Data
A CIP catalogue record for this book is available
from the Library of Congress

British Library Cataloguing in Publication Data
A CIP catalogue record for this book
is available from the British Library

ISBN 1 85302 328 0

Typeset by EMS Phototypesetting, Berwick on Tweed
Printed and bound by The Cromwell Press, Melksham, Wiltshire

Contents

Part A: Introduction

1 Partnership under the Children Act 1989 – an overview

Felicity Kaganas

Partnership under the Children Act 1989 is an elusive and at times chimerical creature. The notion of partnership, which finds expression in exhortations to all concerned with child welfare and protection to work together, as well as in the statutory endorsement of co-operation and non-intervention, appears to have the potential to transform practice relating to child welfare and protection. And yet, on closer examination, when it comes to actually putting partnership into effect, it is not always clear what partnership means or how it can be implemented to accomplish that transformation.

Although there is no mention of partnership in the Act, it is replete with references to co-operation and consultation which are interpreted as embodying different aspects of the principle. Also, partnership is explicitly promoted in the Guidance and Regulations that followed in the wake of the legislation. It seems that partnership, a concept that was already beginning to feature strongly in other spheres such as health and education, was seized upon by those framing the new law as the key to dealing with a whole range of sometimes contradictory pressures. Most of the pressure was generated by criticisms of the previous system and the Act seeks to remedy what were seen to be failings in the provision of services to families in difficulties as well as defects in the child protection process.[1] It represents a response to the disquiet, aroused by cases such as those of Jasmine Beckford and Kimberley Carlile,[2] about the effectiveness of the child protection machinery. It is also the product of the critical consensus following the Cleveland case where social workers were censured for excessive interventionism. It is a statute passed at a time when 'consumer choice' was in the ascendancy and when terminology like 'service providers' and 'users' was entering into the vocabulary of public service organisations. And finally, it was passed at a time when perceptions of children were changing and the notion of

1

children's rights was gaining currency.

These diverse influences, operating to fashion the legislation as well as the Guidance and Regulations, are reflected in the diversity of the different forms of partnership advocated.

- The child abuse enquiries, which drew attention to failures in communication and co-operation between the various agencies involved in child protection, led to an emphasis on partnership between those agencies. As a result, the partnership principle is considered crucial in shaping the relationships between statutory and voluntary bodies; between responsible authorities and the police; between social services and other local authority departments; and between a number of other professionals and organisations.[3]

- The new respect accorded to children's views in *Gillick*[4] and by proponents of children's rights, coupled with the assertion by Lord Justice Butler-Sloss that 'the child is a person and not an object of concern' (Butler-Sloss, 1988:245), gave impetus to the endorsement of a different notion of partnership: partnership with children.

- The Cleveland report, together with the growing tendency to treat social services clients as consumers as well as the increasingly influential concept of the responsible parent, all combined to mandate a third form of partnership: partnership with parents. This, in turn, has been expanded to cover other members of the family and other important figures in the child's life.[5]

- The image of the 'responsible parent' also underlies yet another kind of partnership: the co-operation between parents promoted by the Act.[6]

- There is also said to be a partnership relationship between courts and local authorities.

The practical implications of working in partnership differ in all these situations. Partnership as a concept, therefore, chameleon-like, changes hue depending on the identity of the partners concerned. What is more, 'partnership' is used to denote such a variety of relationships, some of them highly conflicted, that at times, the search for its substance seems like a quest for the holy grail. For it can be questioned whether, in some of the situations in which the term is invoked, partnership in any meaningful sense is possible at all.

The difficulty of translating the partnership principle into practice suggests that its ideological appeal is rather more significant than its usefulness as a basis for a practical framework to secure children's welfare. This book attempts to explore beyond the rhetoric and to examine, in a number of different contexts, what partnership is, whether it can be given practical expression and, if so, how.

Definitions of partnership

That there are problems in translating the partnership principle into more concrete form is readily apparent from the attempts of some writers to describe it; the definitions proffered are characterised by their nebulousness. So, for example, one writer suggests that partnership means 'having to do with the welfare of people in a community' (Aldgate, 1991:5).

More specifically, in relation to inter-agency partnership, *Working Together*[7] states:

'The protection of children requires a close working relationship between social services departments, the police service, medical practitioners, community health workers, schools, voluntary agencies and others. Cooperation at the individual case level needs to be supported by joint agency and management policies for child protection. There must be a recognised joint forum for developing, monitoring and reviewing child protection policies.' (DoH, 1991i:para.1.9)

In relation to partnership generally, encompassing also partnership with families, broader definitions have been essayed. Jo Tunnard of the Family Rights Group asserts confidently:

'The essence of partnership is sharing. It is marked by respect for one another, role divisions, rights to information, accountability, competence and value accorded to individual input. In short, each partner is seen as having something to contribute, power is shared, decisions are made jointly, and roles are not only respected but are also backed by legal and moral rights.' (Tunnard, 1991:1)

However, she goes on to concede that partnership under the Act cannot always live up to this definition: 'It is... difficult for families to be partners of social workers in the complete sense' (Tunnard, 1991:2). So, one is tempted to agree with Ann Buchanan who says ruefully:

'What does working in partnership under the Children Act mean? I thought I knew last week, but maybe now you need to ask me next year.' (Buchanan, 1994:116)

Partnership and the law

In order to discover in any greater detail what might be included under the rubric of partnership, the starting point must be an examination of the Act along with the Guidance and Regulations. These combine to sketch out the main partnership relationships envisaged and, at times, the broad outlines of the areas in which the partners are to work together. For instance, the legislation contains provisions intended to ensure that the various agencies engaged in child protection work in partnership with each other. One of the sections formulated for this purpose, for instance, instructs local authorities to co-operate with one another, and with local education authorities, local housing authorities and health authorities.[8] Other provisions are designed to promote partnership with families. Most importantly, the principle of partnership with parents gives substance to the rule that they always retain their parental responsibility and that, even when their child is in care, they can be restrained from exercising it only in limited circumstances.[9] Local authorities are enjoined to seek court orders 'only when this is better for the child than working with parents under voluntary arrangements' (DoH, 1991i:para.1.4); partnership works best where relationships are voluntary and co-operative. Partnership with children is encouraged by prescribing that local authorities ascertain and give due consideration to children's wishes relating to the accommodation provided for them by local authorities.[10]

Other illustrations abound. The partnership principle is reflected in provisions such as sections 22, 61 and 64, imposing a duty on responsible authorities to consult parents, the child concerned and others before making decisions affecting a child being looked after by a local authority, or who is accommodated by a voluntary organisation or in a registered children's home.[11] Partnership also explains the regulations governing cases where a child is looked after or accommodated by a responsible authority; the arrangements must be recorded in writing and 'so far as reasonably practicable' be agreed after consultation with the child, the parents and other relevant individuals and agencies.[12] Similarly, in the event of a review, the views of parents, the child and others must be sought and be taken into account 'unless it is not reasonably practicable to do so'.[13] Finally, s26(3) also facilitates partnership by demanding the creation of complaints procedures for the benefit, amongst others, of parents and children.[14]

From a reading of all the legislation and guidance, a hazy picture of what is envisaged by partnership begins to emerge. It is a collage of rights, duties and recommendations, only some of which are grounded in practice. A great deal of use is made of terms such as 'co-operation' and 'consultation', terms that are vague, that leave considerable room for interpretation and that can mean different things in different situations. As Braye and Preston-Shoot comment in relation to partnership in community care: 'Whilst providing the rhetoric, legislative guidance is short on the practice technology' (1994:174).

Clearly then, defining partnership is beset by difficulties. Not surprisingly, this uncertainty makes its implementation problematic. And even to the extent that we think we understand what is required, working in partnership is no simple matter.

Working in partnership

Inter-agency partnership

The complexities of partnership between different agencies have now become evident. The partnership relationship is affected by the power relations between the social work profession and other professions such as law, medicine and the police (Webb and McBeath, 1989:496). It is also affected by the methods employed to establish co-operative relationships. A Director of Child Care at Barnardo's complains that the contract culture prevailing among organisations offering child care services is incompatible with partnership. Voluntary bodies might find themselves excluded from planning projects and being invited merely to submit tenders. They might find themselves caught up primarily with responding to approaches from local authorities and others without initiating their own projects. He concludes that, in an increasingly commercial climate, working together 'does not feel like a partnership in the same way at all. The concept of purchaser/provider is not the same as a joint and shared approach' (Jarman, 1993:337).

In addition, inter-agency co-operation can be hindered by difficulties such as contradictory statutory duties[15] and divergent priorities (Tunstill, 1991:v; Jarman, 1993:338; Bell and Daly, 1992: 257). For instance, a shared understanding of the category 'children in need', has been cited as a prerequisite for 'appropriate collaborative practice' between statutory and voluntary organisations (Jenkins, 1991:231). Yet research suggests that no such understanding exists. Since lack of resources forces social services to target their efforts on particular groups, such as children at risk, voluntary organisations are placed in a dilemma. Their open access approach does not correspond with social services' narrower focus (Tunstill, 1991:v).

A different problem arises from the requirement that the numerous agencies involved in any case are obliged to inform one another of any developments. This can lead to daunting formalities and a welter of paperwork. The result might be that the accessibility of services and the informal nature of voluntary accommodation in particular, so important for partnership with families, are undermined (Neary, 1991:iii). Measures such as written notification, reviews and the drawing up of health-care plans can leave parents feeling marginalised.

While there are clearly some problems with inter-agency partnership, it is partnership with family members that probably presents the greatest challenge both from the point of view of ascertaining its scope and in putting it into practice. The potential for conflict with parents and other family members is great, particularly when children are considered to be at risk. And for children, partnership is likely to stop short of professionals relinquishing their decision-making powers to promote individual autonomy.

Partnership with children

The Act contains a number of provisions requiring consultation with children[16] and children's wishes are also accorded recognition in the welfare checklist[17] and in the sections entitling children to refuse to submit to psychiatric and medical examinations.[18] However, the statute merely directs that a child's wishes should be one of the factors taken into consideration in making decisions; it does not allow children full self-determination.

Ascertaining what the child's wishes are is not always a simple procedure. One research study (Hodges, 1994) reveals considerable variations among psychologists in identifying the most important factors, for example suggestability or parental pressure, for the purposes of establishing children's views. What is more, although the legislation stipulates that the weight to be given to the child's wishes must be decided in the light of his or her age and understanding, only a minority of the psychologists interviewed gave priority to these considerations. So the law appears to be at odds with professional opinion and is described critically by psychologists as over-simplifying a very difficult and complicated issue.

Not only is the rhetoric of partnership vulnerable to a charge of over-simplification, it is also particularly misleading in this context. The statutory reference to the child's age and understanding echoes the mature minor test enunciated in *Gillick*. The decisions that have followed that case, applying the mature minor test, have severely limited its potential for enhancing children's autonomy.[19] It is instructive to examine these cases, as well as precedent interpreting the Children Act, in order to get an impression of the way in which partnership with children is likely to be viewed. Although *Gillick* and the subsequent decisions deal with consent to medical or psychological assessment or treatment, the principles they establish can be extrapolated to other kinds of decisions.

In *Re R (a Minor) (Wardship: Consent to Treatment)*[20] it was said, *obiter*, that both the court and the parents were entitled to override a Gillick-competent child's refusal to undergo medical treatment. This principle was confirmed in *Re W (a Minor) (Medical Treatment)*[21] where the court stressed the welfare of the child and indicated that the child would be given decision-making powers only to the extent that this could be regarded as prudent. The welfare of the child was again the decisive consideration in *South Glamorgan County Council v W and B.*[22] While the court felt constrained to admit that the minor in question had sufficient understanding to make an informed decision, it invoked its inherent jurisdiction to override her refusal to undergo assessment and treatment in a secure unit. The right to refuse examinations and other kinds of assessment conferred on minors by the Act was held not to affect the court's powers.

These cases suggest that a paternalistic stance is likely to be adopted in relation to decision-making by minors. The fact that the welfare principle is paramount[23] makes this almost inevitable. Although the child's wishes and feelings are included in the checklist,[24] they are not decisive. First, it is always open to workers, as well as courts, who consider the child's wishes unreasonable and irresponsible, to take the view that the child's understanding of all the implications of his or her choice is inadequate. And, second, even if the child does appear to have a good understanding of the situation, the preference expressed by that child can be overridden to ensure that his or her welfare, as construed by the professionals involved, is not jeopardised.

This is not to question the propriety of this approach. Rather, it is to question the appropriateness of the label 'partnership' in these circumstances. A teenager bent on avoiding a proposed course of treatment was compelled to undergo it because, in the local authority's view, confirmed by the court, it was in her best interests to do so. Refusal to co-operate led, first, in *W and B*, to a care order and then to court backing for treatment. The minor's wishes were canvassed but then overruled.

Partnership with parents

The Review of Child Care Law (1985), which preceded the Children Act and which sheds some light on the intentions behind it, reveals considerable concern for the way in which parents were dealt with by the law at that time. It suggests that the majority of children are best looked after by their families and that parents should be allowed to fulfil their 'natural' and 'legal' responsibilities (DHSS, 1985:para.2.8). Since families are the best place for raising children, it says, there should be greater co-operation and openness with parents as well as greater accountability to them.

This philosophy permeates the Act which evinces a clear preference for voluntary and co-operative relationships between social services and parents. The legislation, it is said, 'strikes a new balance between family autonomy and the protection of children' (DoH, 1989b:iii). This new balance is perceptible in the abolition of the parental rights resolution procedure,[25] the scrapping of the requirement that parents give notice before removing a child[26] and in the enactment of the non-intervention principle.[27] Under the new dispensation, compulsory intervention in the family is to be kept to a minimum. Local authorities have a duty to promote the upbringing of children within their families and, in order to facilitate this, to provide support for the families of children in need.[28] This extends to providing accommodation for children in need[29] in a way that does not stigmatise the parents and which does not curtail their parental responsibility.[30] As the White Paper setting out the basis of the Act states, local authority accommodation should:

> be seen in a wider context and as part of a range of services a Local Authority can offer to parents and families in need of help with the care of their children. Such a service should, in appropriate circumstances be seen as a positive response to the needs of families and not as a mark of failure either on the part of the family or those professionals and others working to support them. An essential characteristic of this service should be its voluntary character, that it should be based clearly in continuing parental agreement and operate as far as possible on a basis of partnership and co-operation between the local authority and parents. (DHSS, 1987: para.21)

Even where there is some risk to a child, the policy is to try to avoid taking coercive measures. Schedule 2 of the Act[31] provides that every local authority should take reasonable steps designed to reduce the need for compulsory intervention. The Guidance and Regulations state that where there is a risk, the local authority is obliged to consider whether voluntary accommodation is sufficient to safeguard the child's safety:[32]

> In the majority of cases local authorities will be able to agree on an arrangement that will best provide for the needs of the child....Work with parents to achieve an initial agreement to the accommodation of the child by the local authority will usually ensure that the ongoing plan for the child can be operated in partnership with the parents. (DoH, 1991e:para.2.30)

The import of non-interventionism and the commitment to partnership is that children should be left within the family unless it is absolutely imperative to remove them. And even if they are removed, a partnership relationship should be maintained. For example, parents should still be entitled to have contact with their children[33] and to have a say in their upbringing.[34] Parents retain their parental responsibility.

It is this concept of parental responsibility that is the linchpin of the partnership ideology. Described by some as an 'instrument of social policy' (Edwards and Halpern, 1992:113), it signals a retreat of the state and an endorsement of the 'principles of *laissez faire* individualism and self-sufficiency, the twin guiding tenets of recent Conservative governments' (Edwards and Halpern, 1992: 119).[35] However there is more to the notion of parental responsibility than this. Eekelaar distinguishes between two facets of the concept. The first is responsibility in the sense that child care belongs to the parent rather than the state. The second is responsibility in the sense of the duties parents have to their children (Eekelaar, 1991:37). Expanding on this distinction, it can be argued that responsibility in the first sense, the withdrawal of the state, is made possible by the prevailing assumption that responsibility in the second sense is in fact met by parents, that parents are indeed dutiful and responsible. The image of the responsible parent is constructed on the basis of the belief that parents know and do what is best for their children. Left to their own devices, or perhaps with some unintrusive help, they will competently fulfil their obligations and get on with the job of raising their children. As Murray Ryburn suggests, plans for children need 'to acknowledge that workers do not hold a monopoly on knowing best' (Ryburn, 1991a:15). This policy of liberating and empowering the responsible parent underlies the ideology of partnership. Unless strict grounds are satisfied, parents should continue to be the decision-makers.

Because partnership rests on the assumption that parents are responsible and reasonable, difficulties ensue when they do not conform to this model. Its foundations undermined, the edifice begins to totter. Partnership may become impossible or inappropriate. Judith Harwin warns that actual and suspected abusers frequently suffer from problems like depression, substance abuse and low impulse controls which preclude proper consideration of children's needs. She also notes that the personal and social difficulties affecting the parents can 'sabotage' joint planning. 'No-one should underestimate the difficulties of working in partnership with actual or suspected abusers' (Harwin, 1992:53).

There are two very serious obstacles to meaningful partnership with parents. On one hand, if workers cling too faithfully to its tenets in practice, partnership might place children at risk. And, on the other hand, the discourse of partnership might be deployed as rhetoric to mask the very real coercive power that responsible authorities have over families judged to be irresponsible.

The first of these eventualities is addressed by Bainham. He expresses concern that partnership in the context of voluntary arrangements diminishes local authority control (Bainham, 1990b: 233) and refers to complaints that, generally, 'the legislation has at least as much to do with defending the parental position as it has to do with protecting the welfare of children' (Bainham, 1990d:144). His worry is that this valorization of parenthood imperils the effective operation of the welfare principle. His concerns are echoed by the Children Act Advisory Committee which reports being notified that some local authorities might feel inhibited from applying for care orders, and courts from granting them, unless the partnership potential of the relationship with the family has been exhausted. The Committee warns that delay in taking action can lead to children suffering increased harm.[36]

An empirical study into the incidence of sexual abuse in Leeds also highlights concerns that children are not being well served (Frothingham et al., 1993). This research compared a cohort of children diagnosed as sexually abused after the Cleveland enquiry, when workers began to adapt their practice to anticipate the move towards partnership,[37] with a group who had been diagnosed a few years earlier. It revealed that the later group suffered more severe abuse but that fewer of those children were registered as abused or taken into care. The researchers suggest that this may reflect a conscious policy of avoiding conflict with families and of supporting child care within the family. They contend, however, that a 'significant number of victims did not receive adequate protection' (Frothingham et al., 1993:33).

Fears that children's safety is being compromised are fortified by anecdotal evidence circulating among professionals who claim to have witnessed an increase in serious injuries, such as head injuries and fractures, and re-abuse.[38] While this could be attributed to problems such as unemployment and economic hardship, we cannot discount the possibility that workers, infused with the spirit of partnership, may be too hesitant to intervene in the face of parental objections.

Social workers are acutely conscious of their obligation to give parents a chance to prove themselves. At the same time, if they feel intervention is necessary, whereas previously they might have instituted wardship proceedings, they are now compelled to hold back until they have built up sufficient evidence for a care order.[39] They may also be reluctant to institute proceedings unless they are fairly confident they will succeed lest, if the order is refused, they will be placed in the position of having to try to work in partnership with a hostile and distrustful family.[40]

Of course, partnership and the non-intervention principle were designed specifically to inhibit workers from interfering too readily in the family and to empower parents against the incursions of officialdom. It could be argued that the fault lies not with the concept of partnership but with the professionals putting it into practice. Although misjudgements might endanger some children, this should not alter the principle that it is only when a crisis point is reached that coercive intervention becomes legitimate.

But even if this reasoning were accepted, there remains the second issue which is less easily dismissed: partnership may have the effect of rendering power imbalances invisible. It is the professionals who define when the crisis point justifying intervention is reached. It is the professionals who decide whether parents are irresponsible or unreasonable. In the light of these powers, the question arises whether there is any real substance to the notion of partnership with parents or whether it amounts to no more than rhetoric.

While parents might be accorded more of a voice since the enactment of the Children Act, while they might be consulted and listened to, it is difficult to accept the appellation 'partnership'. Partnership surely implies the existence of common goals? Partnership surely entails every partner having a stake in the success of the joint enterprise?

It could be argued that the parties do have a common goal: securing the child's best interests. But this would be too sanguine a view. Often there is no such consensus. Abusing parents do not necessarily rank their children's welfare as a priority. Alternatively, this common goal might indeed be present but there may also be irreconcilable differences on how to achieve it; families and professionals might disagree as to what best serves children's interests.

In reality, the relationship between the supposed partners is often one of adversaries. The professionals involved are in many cases working with the objective or removing a child perceived to be at risk while the parents are doing their utmost to prevent this. And even in those cases where the parties do unambiguously subscribe to a common objective, to keep the family together, the professionals stand to lose little should this joint enterprise fail. By contrast, the stakes for parents and children are enormous.

Another peculiarity of partnership in child protection cases is that not all the parties have the freedom to choose whether to enter into a partnership relationship. It is the professional partners who decide whether it is fitting to extend an offer of partnership to the family members. On the basis of their assessment of the family, they decide whether partnership is possible and, if so, to what extent. They also largely determine the tasks that family members must perform in order to sustain the partnership. In all this, they are free to discount the views and wishes of their supposed partners. But a rebellious family that refuses to work with the professionals or attempts to ignore their views will find that it cannot safely do so; it will simply be subjected to coercive measures. For those judged irresponsible and unreasonable, the partnership, if it exists at all, will be of the most rudimentary nature. Clearly, then, the partnership is largely controlled by the professional partners.[41]

So, the language of partnership can be misleading if it conveys the impression of a joint undertaking freely embarked upon. It is perhaps disingenuous to declare that there is nothing in the concept of partnership that requires equality between the partners.[42] As Webb and McBeath say:

> [The] language of contract, co-operation and negotiation stands for the notions that each participant, client and social worker, has rationality, is formally equal to the other, and has the respect of the other. (Webb and McBeath, 1989:493)

This moral discourse, they go on, obscures the power relations between social worker and client (Webb and McBeath, 1989:496). Clients are expected to co-operate and modify their behaviour according to the standards purveyed by the professionals (Webb and McBeath, 1989:503-4).[43] If they do not do so, the consequences are serious. Paradoxically, the power of social workers increases with their failures. Recalcitrance and resistance justify further intervention until, finally, a choice has to be made: the client either conforms to the prescribed norms or earns the label of deviant (Harris and Webb, 1987:76).[44]

Frequently, professionals opt for compulsory measures when a point is reached where it is deemed 'impossible to work with' the parents.[45] Although the level of immediate danger to the child within the family has not necessarily increased, the lack of co-operation, obstructing the workers' ability to monitor the situation, is seen as placing the child at risk. The parent who resists surveillance ceases to be a responsible parent or a potentially responsible parent and is no longer a suitable candidate for voluntary partnership. This approach is endorsed in the Guidance and Regulations:

> Where a parent is unwilling to co-operate at the outset or becomes unco-operative... the need for care proceedings or emergency protection action should be considered. (DoH, 1991e:para.2.30)

So, in the end, the parents must submit to the power of the professionals and, in the last resort, of the courts. This is not to deny, however, that there is some room for accommodating parents' wishes. There can be some 'realignment of power relations' (Braye and Preston-Shoot, 1992:521). This is achieved, at least to a degree, as a result of employing measures to ensure greater parental participation. The principal means to this end are consultation with parents, inviting them to attend case conferences and the use of social work agreements. However, the significance of these measures in empowering parents depends to a large extent on the way they are implemented.

Consultation

The duty to consult parents enshrined in the Act does not entail a duty to comply with their wishes. For instance, in relation to education, Braun says:

> Working with parents is not simply about parents learning about and supporting the values of the nursery. Nor is it about nurseries learning about and adopting parents' values.... It is about recognizing... that both partners bring equal but different skills to the task; and that both need to listen, learn and change accordingly. (1992:180)

True, even in respect of children subject to care orders, it is intended that parents should be consulted and that the plans for the child's future should be negotiated (Thoburn, 1991a:336-8). In the final analysis, however, the law entitles parents to be heard and no more. As Ryburn observes:

> The requirements of the Act to consult the views of children and their families could be met and their views recorded, but the process of consultation would mean nothing unless these were the views that workers did their utmost to give expression to in practice. (1991b:11)

In many cases a polite hearing is all that will be accorded to parents; it is difficult to imagine a parent's wishes carrying much weight when opposing a decision to remove a child into care. Perhaps in relation to the more mundane decisions, a parent's voice might be more persuasive but even then it might be overruled.

Where a child is being accommodated by a local authority, parents who object to any arrangements are in a stronger position; they can simply remove their children.[46] But for those parents seeking respite from child care, this would mean losing the facilities that they presumably feel they need. More importantly, for many parents, it involves risking being labelled unreasonable and so, potentially, candidates for compulsory intervention.

Child protection conferences

Working Together identifies two types of child protection conferences: the initial child protection conference and the child protection review (DoH, 1991i:para.6.1). It recommends that children and 'family adults' be encouraged to attend both types (DoH, 1991i:para.6.23). Apart from exceptional cases, parents should not be excluded (DoH, 1991i:para.6.15) because, if they do not hear what is said about them, they are at a disadvantage.[47] If they are excluded, they should be encouraged to communicate their views to the conference by means of a letter or tape recording (DoH, 1991i: para.6.17).

The document cautions that the participation of families in these conferences will not be effective unless they are fully involved from the outset in all stages of the child protection process and unless there is as much openness and honesty as possible between the family and the professionals (DoH, 1991i: para.6.11). It suggests that parents should be permitted to bring with them friends or supporters (DoH, 1991i:para.6.18), implicitly recognising their vulnerability stemming from lack of confidence, inarticulacy or inexperience. The parents and the child are the only ones who are not professionals and are not backed up by a specialist agency (Williams, 1992:71). They need additional support since they are in all likelihood 'one-shotters' against a roomful of 'repeat players'.[48] Families are confronted with a formidable array of people all with the authority conveyed by their titles and by their mastery of a body of specialist knowledge validating their opinions.

Although parents can disrupt conferences or persuade the professionals to consider alternative courses of action to those proposed,[49] ultimately, they may have to accept a decision that is imposed on them. Research in Rochdale shows a significant 'mismatch' between parents' expectations and their experience of conferences (Rochdale ACPC, 1993:paras.10.5-10.6). Parents questioned for the purposes of the study identified as one of their main aims in attending, 'to influence decisions'. However, afterwards, although 45 percent of those interviewed felt they had managed this, an equal number said their presence had made no difference at all. Thoburn, writing elsewhere, concedes that partnership implying shared aims may not be possible in the early stages of most child protection cases, but regards parental participation at conferences as important in order to facilitate the development of partnership as the case proceeds (Thoburn, 1992:14).

Social work agreements

Social work agreements can be deployed for a variety of purposes and with a variety of results. Often, they are intended, among other things, to clarify roles, to obviate hidden agendas, to increase professional accountability and to redress the imbalance of power by enabling parents to negotiate (Braye and Preston-Shoot, 1992: 512).[50] However, they can also be seen as control mechanisms. Social workers interviewed by Nelken, admittedly prior to the implementation of the Act, laid most stress on the practical advantages of agreements in keeping parents to their promises and in keeping arrangements running smoothly. Less was said about respect for clients and social work accountability (Nelken, 1987: 218).

Although not referred to in the Act, written social work agreements are required explicitly or in some cases, implicitly, by the regulations.[51] The Guidance and Regulations relating to family placements makes it clear that it is expected, where the child is not in care, that a child-care plan be devised with the parents' agreement (DoH, 1991f:paras.2.63-2.67). Where the child is placed in accommodation, this plan should form the basis of a written agreement with the parents. If there is 'non co-operation' on the parents' part, it is stated that their agreement to the arrangements for their children can be dispensed with. So again, resistance by parents may be taken to signify that they are unreasonable with the result that they are marginalised.

Clearly, those who do consent to participate in drawing up an agreement may be induced to do so under considerable pressure. The possible sanctions should they refuse are severe: 'It's a brutal choice and the choice may be work with us or lose your child.'[52] As far as the terms of the agreement are concerned, these are not freely negotiable. In effect, the parents want to keep their children and the agreement tells them what conditions they have to satisfy in order to do so (Nelken, 1987:214,227). The authority of the professionals generated by their status and specialist knowledge is backed up by their statutory power to ensure that their norms prevail. And the way in which the agreement is implemented might also be affected by this imbalance of power. As Rojek and Collins point out, merely because there is agreement on matters like arrangements to meet, 'there is no guarantee that what happens in these sessions will be genuinely non-authoritarian, non-judgemental and participative' (1987:203).

Finally, in the event of parental failure to comply with the agreement, this failure can be taken as evidence of their irresponsibility. Material documenting parents' shortcomings might form the basis of court reports (Rojek and Collins, 1987:209) and may be used to justify a decision approving removal of their child. In these circumstances, the agreement functions as a test to determine the suitability of the parents. Sometimes, Nelken observes, this test is designed to make the parents fail. When they do, this is offered as proof to the parent and to the court of parental deficiency (Nelken, 1988:116-7).

Putting partnership in context

The notion of partnership under the Children Act is far removed from our ordinary understanding of the word. It evokes a warm glow, suggesting that professionals and families alike are striving for the same ideal: the welfare of children. But it hides a multitude of problems. It cloaks the difficult choices that have to be made by professionals and denies their power. At the same time it creates an unrealistic image of the family. As Staines remarks:

> The right's fantasy of ideal families and the left's romantic notion of the ideal poor would have us enter a new world of double-think in which we will be required to pretend that all people are decent, well-motivated, and capable, while knowing that people become clients through indecency, ill-intention, or incapacity. (1991:ii)

In short, it reduces the overwhelming complexity of protecting children while respecting families to a single, seemingly simple concept. It is important not to be seduced by its promise of amicable consensus.

In order to achieve a coherent response to calls for partnership, it is necessary to penetrate behind the ideology. It is important to unpick the concept of partnership, to consider the possibilities in any situation for implementing it and to acknowledge that it is not a panacea for all ills.

This book is intended to contribute to that process. The authors examine partnership in a number of different contexts, exploring the policies and ideologies that underlie it, the way it works in practice and its potential to improve work with families and children. The book is divided into three main parts.

- The first locates the concept of partnership within a legal framework and considers the implications of the law for both families and professionals.

- The second part approaches partnership from the perspective of professionals engaged in working with children and families.

- The third is made up of explications of partnership within particular theoretical paradigms.

In the first part, Judith Masson sets out to unravel the concept of partnership and to move beyond the circumscribed framework provided by the law. She examines what professionals mean by it and identifies the legitimate expectations of the parents with whom they work. She points to the parents' needs, such as the need for access to information, the need for participation in decision-making in environments that are not intimidating to reduce the risk of one-sided negotiations, and the need for a right to complain and reject help. On the basis of these considerations, she evaluates the possibilities of partnership in the spheres of housing, special education, child protection and 'lost parents'. She concludes that the Children Act imposes only minimum requirements for potential involvement and that more could be done to change relationships between families and professionals.

Christine Piper's chapter approaches partnership from a slightly different perspective, that of partnership between parents. She sets out to show how assumptions made by professionals about the relationships between mothers, fathers, children and others affect decisions about providing services and influence the way welfare workers relate to individual family members. She argues that it is important to confront the fact that some of those who qualify legally as 'partners' (usually fathers), in reality do not play an active part in their childrens' upbringing. That professionals tend to ignore fathers leads to a number of consequences.

- First, fathers who are active parents are marginalised.

- Second, fathers who don't take on any of the burdens of child care escape criticism and pressure to contribute.

- Third, the increased burden on others (usually mothers) is rendered invisible.

Piper maintains that if the parental unit is not seen in gendered terms, sexist practice will not be changed. So mothers rather than fathers will continue to be subject to surveillance and blame. She concludes with a warning that unless these issues are addressed, partnership, instead of functioning as a mechanism for empowering parents, may simply prove to be a way of controlling women.

A comparative view is provided by Alison Diduck who draws parallels between Canadian child protection legislation and the Children Act 1989. She highlights the similarities and differences in the two systems and uncovers the common ideological strands in each jurisdiction that shape the law. She explores the difficulties of working in partnership in the context of policies endorsing privatisation of the family, autonomy and due process for the family, while at the same time monitoring and investigating it with a view to potential coercive action. Partnership as an ideology, she maintains, obscures this tension between helping families and gathering evidence against them.

A more optimistic note is struck by June Thoburn's chapter, suggesting that partnership between social workers and families, at least in some sense, is possible, given sufficient resources, improved training and a professional commitment to working together. She analyses two empirical studies designed to determine, amongst other things, whether the principles in the Act are being followed and the extent to which partnership relationships are being formed. Adopting Tunnard's definition of partnership, she reveals that partnership principles seem rarely to be adhered to in the initial stages of social services involvement; priority is given to protecting children at risk. Nevertheless, in those cases where social services are working with families, she finds that active participation by parents, even in the most unlikely cases, can take place with the aid of skilled social workers and sensitive procedures. And she finds little evidence that children are prejudiced by this.

Brynna Kroll confronts the difficulty of interpreting the partnership principle in the context of the relationship between professionals and children. She points out that the power imbalance between adults and children, as well as children's need for adults to take control in some situations, must colour the way in which professionals work with children. She sets out to devise a 'starter kit' to facilitate the building of a model for child-centred social work. This model is built of four essential components:

- A child-centred philosophy.

- A bank of theoretical knowledge to assist in understanding children's worlds.

- Techniques for communicating with children.

- Appropriate training, supervision and support for social workers.

Partnership, she explains, entails listening to children to assess their needs and deploying the appropriate skills to make sense of what they communicate.

From the viewpoint of a child psychiatrist, partnership looks like a far from rosy prospect. Mark Berelowitz is sceptical, arguing that in cases of child abuse, partnership can have little meaning when applied to the relationship between psychiatrist and family. The concept fails to take into account the psychological implications of an allegation of abuse. In addition, there are other impediments, some structural, to co-operation between professionals and between families and professionals. These include lack of social services resources as well as the adversarial nature of the legal system. The qualities needed for co-operation are largely absent in cases of abuse. Those concerned about the well-being of children would be better advised to shift their partnership efforts from child protection to promoting children's health, welfare and education.

Robin Solomon focuses her attention on structural impediments to partnership. Her chapter examines the relationship between statutory, voluntary and private sector agencies within a purchaser/provider model. She analyses the effect on child protection of the introduction of this market economy model into the organisation of services. She points out that it does not necessarily operate to promote improved quality when applied to the purchase and supply of welfare services. She also argues, relying on research into institutional defences and on the phenomena of splitting and projection, that there may be serious therapeutic disadvantages in allocating the duty to provide welfare services to voluntary agencies and surveillance to statutory agencies. In short, this model, although it might work, has the potential to adversely affect the relationship between the various agencies as well as each agency's relationship with its clients.

Sarah Woodhouse constructs a theoretical framework within which she explores the assumptions underpinning the concept of partnership. She suggests that it is based on particular models of parents and social workers and the way in which they relate to one another. The dominant model underlying partnership is a consensus model and it fails to accord with the reality of child protection casework. Referring to an empirical study she conducted in 1992-3 in three social services departments, Woodhouse reveals that social workers are understandably uncertain about how to put the theory of partnership into practice and whether this should be attempted in child protection cases.

The chapter by Michael King draws on the theoretical framework propounded by Niklas Luhmann which constructs law and politics as distinct, self-referential systems. He notes the current ascendancy of law over other discourses in determining what is required of families in order to secure what is considered a safe and stable society. Part of his explanation for this focuses on the capacity of law, with its coding of events as either lawful or unlawful, to reduce complexity to manageable proportions. Law defines certain types of conduct as abuse and therefore unlawful, while other forms of behaviour are permitted as lawful. The coding of something as abuse legitimates interference with parents' autonomy and the concept of partnership can assist workers in dealing with the imponderables that bedevil the process of assessing whether there is a risk of abuse. Partnership failure is reconstructed by law to raise a presumption of unlawfulness. This tendency of the law to effect such reconstructions is not confined to the courtroom. The dominance of law leads social service workers to use partnership, not so much as a way of maintaining co-operation, but, lest things go wrong, as a device for amassing evidence and proving parental deficiency in court.

Notes

1. See, generally, Parton (1991).
2. See DoH (1991c).
3. See further, for example DoH (1991i); DoH (1989:para.4.37-8); Jenkins (1991:227).
4. *Gillick* v *West Norfolk and Wisbech Area Health Authority* ([1985] 3 All ER 402).
5. See, for example, Braun (1992:178).
6. See Parry (1992:10-11) and Aldgate (1991:5).
7. *Working Together* was published as guidance in terms of s7 of the Local Authority Social Services Act 1970. It does not have the force of statute but should be complied with in the absence of exceptional circumstances justifying deviation from it.
8. Section 27 Children Act 1989. See, generally, Jenkins (1991: 227ff).
9. See s33 Children Act 1989. See also, DoH (1991f:para.2.10).
10. Section 20(6) Children Act 1989.
11. Idem.
12. Regulation 3, Arrangements for Placement of Children (General) Regulations 1991.
13. Regulation 7, Review of Children's Cases Regulations 1991; s26(2)(d) Children Act 1989.
14. See, generally, Ryan (1991:167ff).
15. See, for example, Neate (1991:12ff).
16. See, for example, s22 Children Act 1989.
17. Section 1(3) Children Act 1989.
18. Section 43(8) and s44(7) Children Act 1989.
19. See, generally, Montgomery (1993).
20. (1992) 1 *FLR* 190.
21. (1992) *Fam Law* 541.
22. (1993) 1 *FLR* 574.
23. Section 1(1) Children Act 1989.
24. Section 1(3) Children Act 1989.
25. In terms of s3 Child Care Act 1980.
26. This was contained in s13(2) Child Care Act 1980.
27. Section 1(5) Children Act 1989.
28. Section 17 Children Act 1989.
29. Section 20 Children Act 1989.
30. The only powers that can be exercised by the local authority are those that are delegated to them by the parents or the power to do what is reasonable in terms of s3(5).
31. Paragraph 7.

32. See also DoH (1989:para.1.9); Thoburn (1991b:109).
33. Section 34 Children Act 1989.
34. See, for example, DoH (1991c:62-3).
35. See also Eekelaar (1991).
36. The Children Act Advisory Committee, Annual Report 1992/3, 33-4.
37. Dr Christopher Hobbs, St James University Hospital, Leeds (personal communication, 21 June 1994).
38. This increase was referred to by a community paediatrician, Dr Jane Watkeys (Panel member, 'Partnership: Raising the Issues', Conference: Partnership Under the Children Act 1989: Two Years On, 22 Sept 1993, Brunel University in association with the Tavistock Clinic). The prevalence in many parts of the country of the belief that serious injuries are more common was confirmed by Mr K. Watson, custodian of the Child Protection Register in Leeds (personal communication, 17 June 1994). Dr Jane Wynne, a Consultant Community Paediatrician working in Leeds, said she has seen an increase in physical abuse and that head injuries and fractures have become more common (personal communication, 21 June 1994).
39. Christine Bridgett, social worker with children and families, (personal communication, 10 May 1994).
40. Personal notes of workshops.
41. See also Archer and Whitaker (1992:66).
42. See Aldgate, Tunstill and Atherton (1991:262) and Tunnard (1991:5).
43. See also Donzelot (1980).
44. See also Webb and McBeath (1989:495).
45. This observation is based on the writer's personal notes on numerous workshops.
46. Section 20(8) Children Act 1989.
47. See, for example, Atherton (1991:188).
48. See Galanter (1974-5).
49. See, for example, Isaac (1991:206).
50. See also Nelken (1987:215-7).
51. See Braye and Preston-Shoot (1992:512).
52. NSPCC inspectors quoted by Nelken (1988:119).

Part B: Legal frameworks for partnership

2 Partnership with parents: doing something together under the Children Act 1989

Judith Masson

'Working in Partnership' has risen as the slogan of the 'caring 1990s' supplanting children's rights both in its over-use and its search for a definition (DHSS, 1986:para 2.6). A wide range of different relationships within social welfare are all labelled as 'partnerships' suggesting that there are common goals which ensure that both parties are likely to be satisfied with the processes and resulting outcomes. Partnerships are, for example, said or expected, to exist:

- Between social workers or social services departments and parents, children and foster carers (DoH 1990:8).

- Between social services departments and other authorities or other local authority departments such as education, housing and leisure services which also have some responsibilities to families.

- Between local authorities and the voluntary organisations to which they provide grants or enter into service contracts.

- Between courts and local authorities over decision-making in child care.[1]

Parents are the partners not only of social workers but also of doctors (Report of the Committee on Child Health Services, 1976) and schools (DES, 1992:7), but these partnerships with professionals may in practice have only superficial similarity so that parental expectations raised in one setting may not be met in another.

This chapter attempts to unravel the concept of partnership and explore its constituent parts to establish what professionals mean by it and to determine the legitimate expectations of the parents with whom they are working. Only if it is clear what partnership is and what the effects it is meant to have on service delivery are, can its existence be noted, its effectiveness be assessed and its shortcomings be identified. Training for partnership must address the specific knowledge and skills bases for the particular working relationship otherwise those expected to engage in partnership will not know what they need to do nor how to embark upon it.

A short history of partnership

Although earlier calls for partnership with parents came from health and education, such calls are relatively recent in relation to social work. The Report of the Committee on Child Health Services in 1976, *Fit for the Future*, recommended that professionals should see themselves as 'partners with parents: prepared and willing to give them explanations and advice about their child's health'. Health care professionals needed to break down barriers between themselves and parents, change their attitudes and improve communication so that parents would not feel they were 'passive by-standers rather than active partners' (para. 5.6) in their care of children.

Change has not been instantaneous nor has it been driven only by a wish to improve parents' and children's experience of health care. However there have been marked changes in the provision of child health services (DoH, 1991e:1). Parents have been included in the care of children in hospital, although proper facilities are not always available, (Audit Commission, 1993) and many now participate in a scheme through which they hold the child's health records. The Patient's Charter, rights to choose a G.P. and to complain, as well as the existence of the Health Service Ombudsman have redressed the imbalance in professional power to a small degree but parents have found it necessary to turn to the courts when treatment has been refused or operations cancelled because a specialist unit has been closed without consultation.[2] Parents who experience long waits for treatment for their children and abrupt or uncommunicative staff may not feel that they are treated as partners but, by comparison with earlier years, some progress seems to have been made. There are also examples of medical staff going to considerable lengths to find a treatment regime for a sick child which parents can support. For example, in one reported case the earliest treatment of the child's leukaemia was without blood products because of the parents' religious beliefs. Only when the child's condition worsened and following considerable negotiation was the decision placed before the court.[3]

The relationship between parents and schools has also changed markedly over the last 20 years (Wolfendale, 1988). In the past parents were virtually excluded from schools, invited only for special occasions or summoned by the head teacher if problems occurred. Now schools are required to provide a range of information to parents and most rely heavily on parents outside and inside the classroom (see Piper, p.41-5). Some parents have a formal role in school management including responsibilities for the budget as school governors.

The Warnock Report which led to the Education Act 1981 included a chapter headed 'Parents as Partners' explaining the necessity for partnership for the successful education of special needs children:

> 'professional help cannot be wholly effective – if at all so – unless it builds on the parents' own understanding of their children's needs and upon the parents' capacity to be involved....Parents can be effective partners only if professionals take notice of what they say and how they express their needs, and treat their contribution as intrinsically important'. (para. 9.6).

The partnership under the Education Act 1981 allowed these parents to initiate and participate in the assessment process but they had fewer rights over choice of school than other parents. The Parliamentary Education, Science and Arts Committee noted in 1987 their dissatisfaction with the system. The Committee recognised that lack of information, support and choice were common difficulties and that some parents found formal procedures hard to understand and felt that their views were given insufficient weight.[4] Attempts have now been made in the Education Act 1993 to strengthen the position of parents so that they have some rights over choice of school (only within the maintained sector) and better rights of appeal (to an independent tribunal rather than the Secretary of State). Also, in order to control local authority discretion a Statutory Code of Guidance is available which sets criteria for making special needs assessment and issuing statements. However parents still lack support within the process of 'statementing' which was recommended by Warnock and the Parliamentary Committees; concern remains that statements will continue to be based on available resources rather than on children's identifiable needs.[5]

Beyond the framework of special education, partnership with parents has recently received publicity with the re-issue of the Parent's Charter (Department for Education, 1994). However, this followed a period during which politicians used the rhetoric of parents' rights against teachers, their professional bodies and local education authorities. This appears to have raised parental expectations, particularly regarding choice of school, and resulted in a growth of litigation between parents and education authorities rather than a development of co-operation.

Although changing relationships between social workers and their clients was already a concern of radical social work in the 1970s, the issue of partnership really came to the fore in the Barclay Report in 1982. The Report concluded that the personal social services 'need to develop a close working partnership with citizens' (Barclay Report 1982:217). However this was not aimed at empowering clients, but at the development and support of informal care services. Clients' rights needed to be formalised so that individual citizens could gain access to information, participate in decisions, make complaints and obtain second opinions (ibid, 191). The danger that this might lead to more adversarial relations was acknowledged but this was seen as having the potential to strengthen social work.

Partnership and the Children Act 1989

Although developments in the theorising of social work (Rojek et al, 1988) made social workers more aware of the power dimensions in their work in the 1980s, changes in practice in child care during this period were largely responses to child death inquiries and other scandals rather than new professional approaches or changes in the law. Social services departments and the Department of Health responded to the scandals by emphasising the importance of bureaucratic structures, particularly to co-ordinate child protection work. The review of the existing law and preparation of a new legal framework provided the opportunity to consider the relationship between parents, children and the State more broadly and, ultimately, to set a new balance.

The proposals for shared care in the Review of Child Care Law were intended to provide a framework for partnership between parents and local authorities (DHSS, 1985:para.7.1). Voluntary agreement to the provision of care was fundamental to this proposal but the Review did not favour formal 'care agreements'. Parents might be pressured to agree, and individual agreements would lead to variation in legal rights between children, increasing the complexity for carers (para.7.16-17). There was no mention of partnership in relation to compulsory care.

The proposals in the Review of Child Care Law for involving parents were very limited, particularly in comparison with the development in New Zealand of the idea of Family Group Conferences which was introduced in the Children, Young Persons and their Families Act (1989) (Connolly, 1994:87). This New Zealand Act requires the social services authority to arrange a family meeting where family members, without professionals, plan for the child's care. The Director General of Social Welfare is required to provide services to give effect to the decision of the family group conference. Although the Review recommended a 'legislative framework for positive participation' (DHSS, 1985:para.7.23), this was limited to informing and consulting parents on the initial placement and subsequent changes of placement and clarifying the rights (such as choice of school) that they retained. Procedural rights, for example rights to attend meetings or obtain copies of documents, were not considered. Subsequent attempts to legislate such rights were rejected. Regulations were made covering reviews[6] which permit parental attendance but do not mandate it and make it subject to local authority discretion. Case conferences were considered by the Department of Health not to be creatures of statute and this was sufficient to excuse the creation of rights of attendance to these or the many other decision-making fora.

The increased emphasis on partnership was not merely a matter of adopting new beliefs. Research evidence, particularly from Packman and Fisher and their colleagues, called into question both the need for compulsory action in many cases and also the capacity of the child care system to succeed if it failed to respond to requests from parents and excluded them from involvement in the lives of their children in care (Packman et al., 1986; Fisher et al., 1986). The research basis is significant because it provides empirical evidence of the importance of the elements which might constitute partnership.

'Voluntary partnership with parents' became a principle guiding the government approach to the provision of services to children in need and it incorporated the notions of maintaining contact and speedy reunification for children who were cared for away from their homes (DHSS, 1987:para.56). But the term 'partnership' did not appear in the Children Act 1989, nor in the Department of Health introduction to the Act (DoH, 1989b). Volume 2 of the Guidance and Regulations contains the first official definition:

> Partnership requires informed participation. The Act therefore requires that parents and children must be consulted during the decision-making process and notified of the outcome. There is a new requirement placed on local authorities to establish a procedure for considering representations (including complaints) about the discharge of their functions under the Act....Work with parents to achieve an initial agreement to the accommodation of the child by the local authority will usually ensure that the ongoing plan for the child can be operated in partnership with his parents. Where the parent is unwilling... the nature of the arrangements should be reassessed and the need for care proceedings... be considered (DoH, 1991e:para.2.28-9).

It would seem from this that what the Act requires is to be taken to amount to partnership. This contrasts with the notion of partnership as an ideal which should be constantly worked towards which seems to reflect the approach in health and education.

If the Children Act itself establishes 'partnership', any discussion as to how might one improve the parent/social work relationship is blocked until such time as partnership is replaced with a new concept.

Alternative definitions of partnership

Informed participation and an option of complaining would seem a minimalist approach to the concept which would suggest to some a need for common goals and equality within a consensual relation-ship (Armstrong, 1993:21). While the Warnock Report stressed equality as an ideal (Warnock, 1978:para.9.6), it would seem to preclude the use of the term 'partnership' in child care social work. The relationship between a public sector social worker and his or her client can never be one of equality because the social worker's position carries with it powers and duties the exercise of which may affect the client's life contrary to his or her wishes. Social workers are required because of constraints on resources to act as gatekeepers; in child protection work they have specific duties. However, the notion of unequal relationships as 'partnerships' is well established in other areas of social activity. The problem is that by using the term 'partnership' the inequality may be masked and those with power may cease to be concerned about the misuse of such power (Biehal & Sainsbury, 1991:248-9).

The definition of partnership in Volume 2 of the Guidance and Regulations seems to distinguish 'working in partnership' from 'working under court orders' and thus to exclude the parents of children in care from partnership with their social workers. A similar implication can be drawn from the Children Act Report 1992: although this report accepts that the two approaches 'are not mutually exclusive' it repeatedly contrasts working under court orders with working in partnership (DoH/Welsh Office, 1992: para.2.19-21, 2.38). However, according to the Act, there is little difference between the obligations of social workers to parents whether the child is accommodated or in care. In both cases social workers must ascertain their wishes and feelings and give due consideration to them in making any decision (s.22(4)(b) and (5)(b)). The parents of a child in care may not remove the child and their exercise of parental responsibility is curtailed when this is required for the child's welfare (s.33(3)(b) and (4)). Parental agreement to the care arrangements is not required under the Arrangements for Placement of Children (General) Regulations 1991[7] but they can complain about the services provided (s.26) and may apply to the court to have the order discharged (s.39). The fact that parents need not consent to the care arrangements would not, in good practice terms, justify a failure to attempt to involve them, particularly in the light of research evidence which stresses the importance of this to the child's well-being in placement and for reunification (DoH, 1991g).

Lack of freedom within a relationship is only one of the consequences of an imbalance of power. Once it is accepted that partners may not be equal there would seem to be no reason why control of some aspects of their relationship should preclude them from operating in other respects as partners.

Disaggregation of partnership

In *Patterns and Outcomes in Child Placement*, the Department of Health sought to disseminate the major messages from child care research of the 1980s. It noted that there was often no agreement on the nature of the client's problems, there were low levels of parental participation and little use was made of written agreements (DoH, 1991g:40-42). Despite this, social workers frequently considered that they were already working in partnership (Marsh, 1990:30). Four main barriers to partnership were identified:

- Tradition and bureaucracy.

- The level of skill; sensitivity and time required from social workers.

- The parents' personal problems and willingness to co-operate.

- Problems with the balance of power (DoH, 1991g:44).

The Children Act 1989 has made almost no inroads into any of these. The new principle of family support is intended to replace the tradition of child rescue and marginalization of parents but the emphasis on regulations and guidance rather than professionalism and supervision has increased the bureaucracy. Power to terminate contact has been removed from social workers and this and the change in philosophy can be expected to reduce the number of such terminations but the need to respond to court proceedings brought by the local authority is unlikely to be seen by parents as empowering. The courts too seem to support the local authority's plans about contact in preference to parental claims.[8] Social work resources remain stretched. Three percent of children looked after by local authorities in June 1992 were not allocated to a social worker (DoH/Welsh Office, 1992:para.2.59) and thus their parents had no one person with whom to work in partnership.

Attempts to involve parents more in decisions about their children need to focus on the various aspects of looking after children and the part parents can play in this. Parents need to know what is going on in their children's lives to be able to make decisions about them and thus need full information from schools and doctors as well as the children's day-to-day carers. Ideally they should be able to receive that information direct and be able to question the person giving it but, if this is not possible, they need to be confident that it has not been edited. Policies and practices about recording and access to records are therefore crucial. Now that both used and unused material relevant to criminal proceedings must generally be disclosed to the defence, it is hard to justify restrictive approaches to access to records.[9]

The timing and setting for discussions and the form they take are also important. Whether discussions are formal or informal parents need time to prepare and to receive support if they want it. Formal settings such as case conferences, complaints boards and courts can be very intimidating and confusing to those who are unfamiliar with the rules that apply. Anxiety may prevent people attending or inhibit them from taking part. Preparation for such events is essential. Parents need access to general material about agency policy and practice and to independent people who can help them understand this. Wherever possible they should have choices between the various services available for them and their children.

If attempts to reach agreement about problems and solutions are fundamental to a relationship, both parties need to have negotiation skills, not so that one can outwit the other, but so each can contribute fully to the decision reached. There are particular problems for parents seeking accommodation for their child for the first time. They may have little idea what they should expect and what is expected of them. Negotiations to reach a care arrangement may be very one-sided; early relationships may set the tone for the future. Thus knowledge, support and time are crucial. Access to befrienders, particularly parents who have been through the same experience, may be helpful.

Disaggregating partnership does not avoid the problems inherent in the relationship between social workers and parents but requires the former to examine what they are doing to encourage participation and the exercise provides a basis for measuring performance. Each separate aspect clearly requires the support of the employing agencies in establishing policies and funding programmes which will help social workers to develop appropriate skills and their own support systems. Disaggregation also makes it possible to consider the limits to partnership which apply in different contexts. The remainder of this chapter will explore four of these:

- Homelessness.
- Special education.
- Child protection.
- 'Lost parents'.

Homelessness

Local housing authorities owe homeless people with dependent children a duty to provide housing, as long as they are not intentionally homeless.[10] Restrictions on expenditure on new housing and the sale of council housing have reduced the local authority stock so that in some places all new lettings are taken up by homeless people (Audit Commission, 1989). Homeless persons units do not claim to work in partnership with their clients. Their focus is in assessing eligibility within a system based on rationing. Applicants are questioned in detail to verify stories, a procedure which some perceive as demeaning. They are generally given no choice about accommodation and no second chances, and they are provided with very little information about the process, particularly their likely length of stay in temporary accommodation (Niner, 1989: 102). The law gives applicants a right only to have their cases considered by considerate staff.[11] A research report for the DoE concludes:

> The terms of the legislation which determine who qualifies for assistance and the resources available to meet the needs of the qualifying homeless are likely to be the most fundamental determinants of authority/client relations (Niner, 1989:103).

The children of homeless families are likely to be children in need under the Children Act 1989 – a third of authorities used homelessness as an identifier for this category (Aldgate et al., 1992). Homelessness has notoriously been the cause of separation of parents and children through use of 'voluntary care' to meet only the child's accommodation needs. An attempt to preclude that by specific amendment to the Children Bill was unsuccessful and social services departments which do not have housing resources have to rely on negotiations with housing authorities and their power to require co-operation. The statutory Code of Guidance on Homelessness is unhelpful, merely suggesting that policies and procedures for collaboration would be helpful.[12] Although there is some evidence of corporate planning within authorities, the interpretation of s.27[13] indicates the unwillingness of departments within local authorities to be subject to calls from social services. For county councils there is the further problem of needing to reach agreements with a number of district councils each with different policies and resource constraints.

A social work partnership with homeless families is made more difficult by the poor fit between the Children Act 1989 and the Housing Act 1985, limited co-operation in formulating policies and practices and the negative experiences of homeless people in dealing with local authorities. The root cause is inadequate resources and the consequent division of applicants into the worthy and the unworthy (intentionally homeless), a problem which is unlikely to be solved by better training or even joint policies. This problem affects partnership in other contexts too. For example, social services departments face reduced budgets for services to 'children in need'.

Special education

Restrictions on resources to meet special educational needs have influenced the way the Education Act 1981 has been implemented. Some local authorities are reluctant to provide statements on children because they do not wish to incur duties to provide specific facilities (Audit Commission, 1992:1) while others formulate statements of special educational needs to ensure that only existing resources are required. These practices take place under a regime of partnership with parents but have led to increased parental requests for formal statements and use of the courts to ensure provision for their children. The Audit Commission in its report *Getting in on the Act* was critical of the lack of clarity about what constituted 'special educational needs'. It noted that the failure of the Act to define 'special educational need' made it difficult for local education authorities to implement it consistently (Audit Commission, 1992:para.23). Similar comments could be made of the Children Act 1989 in relation to 'children in need'. Although s.17 contains a definition, except for 'disabled children' it is too wide, given the limited resources that are available.

The Audit Commission called for limited parental choice and increased emphasis on responding to parents' wishes (Audit Commission, 1992:paras.133-136). This is provided for in the Education Act 1993 which also empowers the Secretary of State to issue a code of practical guidance about special education and establishes a tribunal to deal with appeals against the contents of statements and refusals to issue statements.[14] It will therefore theoretically be considerably easier for parents to challenge decisions by local education authorities. The tribunal system provides a more effective remedy than the complaints service under the Children Act 1989 because it is fully independent and requires the authority to take specific action. For parents, however, it may be more intimidating. It remains to be seen whether increasing rights in this way will encourage the involvement of less assertive parents.

Child protection

Working in partnership in child protection is not assisted by the frequent restriction of that term to 'voluntary' cases. The separation of the Department of Health sponsored training material on Parts III and IV/V may have been necessary to create manageable programmes but encouraged this distinction. Similarly the lack of material on child protection aimed at senior managers and did not assist the development of policies informed by the research evidence. These difficulties may be remedied over time as experience grows and through the publication in 1995 of the Department of Health 'third pink book' which will disseminate research in child protection.

Partnership in child protection, however, poses further difficulties because of the increased use of the criminal law. Although there is evidence of changes in policy to permit parental participation in case conferences generally (DoH, 1993c:para.1.18), policies of exclusion where a prosecution may occur still exist (for example, Hammersmith and Fulham). Twenty-two percent of Area Child Protection Committee Annual Reports mentioned a policy of full parental attendance at case conferences for 1991-92 compared with five percent for the previous year but it was not clear what proportion of parents actually attended in each of the authorities. Thirty-nine percent of reports mentioned provision of written information to parents which explained formal child protection processes but only nine reports mentioned complaints and appeals procedures, the establishment of which is recommended in *Working Together under the Children Act 1989* (DoH, 1991i:para.6.8-6.13).

The focus on preparing for and completing an interview which satisfies the *Memorandum of Good Practice* (Home Office/DoH, 1992) may also take attention away from work to encourage parental involvement even though only a tiny minority of interviews will lead to proceedings. There is a similar problem with preparing court proceedings. Although there are no legal reasons excluding the parents while proceedings are pending, pressure of work may preclude this. Partnership with parents in child protection is not risk-free: parents may be manipulative and their views may conflict with the child's welfare which is the social worker's primary responsibility. Training and supervision can reduce these risks but social workers need the support of the community in taking this new approach. It is far from clear that the pervading climate of suspicion and blame provides this.

'Lost parents'

The obligations of social service departments to consult and give due consideration to parents' wishes also apply to the parents of children who entered the care system prior to the Children Act 1989, including those whose contact was terminated under the Child Care Act 1980. In these cases the local authority may have no current information about the parents and may not even know their whereabouts. If the parents were unmarried, little information about the father may have been collected when they entered the care system. Although there may be no prospect of children leaving care, it is important for them to have access to knowledge about their family and help to integrate this into their identity (Harrison and Masson, 1994:41). This will be particularly important for children brought up with limited access to their cultural heritage. In order to 'safeguard and promote' the welfare of children who have few links with their families, local authorities should try to involve their parents rather than merely leave the families or the children to take the initiative. There is, however, very little experience in rebuilding relationships between professionals and parents or between parents and children on which to base this work. Social workers too need information about how to trace parents and guidance about making contact with them. In some cases current practice might have led to a different approach but redress will be unlikely. Parents who have coped with the loss of their child cannot be expected to respond willingly to requests to provide information without receiving anything in return.

The forms of parental involvement available will also depend on the child's needs and wishes and the capacities of their current carers. Although it is possible that a few children could return home (Davidson, 1980:52) and that more will establish some contact with parents or other family members, there will be other cases where there are no such positive results. An action research project exploring partnership with 'lost' parents is seeking to address these points (Harrison and Masson, 1994:43).

It requires considerable commitment of time and resources from individual social workers, their team members and their authorities to undertake this work which may be marginalised to a few cases only (Millham et al., 1989) and to children who are likely to move out of the system soon. Preliminary enquiries suggest that some social workers had not realised that partnership also applies to cases pre-dating the Children Act and that some agencies are content to ignore the issue and only respond to parents who actively seek to become involved. Focusing on those who make demands detracts from work designed to encourage participation of all, and at all times, and may lead to more parents being lost despite the new partnership approach in the Children Act 1989.

These four examples would suggest that attention needs to be given to the legal provisions, policy development, resources, attitudes and skills if progress is to be made in involving parents in social work with their children.

Conclusion

There is a clear need to disaggregate the concept of partnership into its constituent parts:

- Respect for the parents' status as persons with parental respons-ibility.

- Participation for parents in decision-making which itself re-quires full access to information, empowerment and support.

- The right to complain, to make choices and to reject help.

Whilst providing a framework which includes most of these elements and allowing some of them to be partly overridden for the protection of children subject to public law court orders, the Children Act 1989 does not place limits on the involvement of parents in their children's upbringing. In imposing duties to consult and providing a framework for complaints it is merely setting minimum requirements and limiting the circumstances where local authority failure can be challenged in the courts. Far more could be done to change the relationship between family service seekers or service users, local authority purchasers and local authority, voluntary organisations or private providers but not without resources which allow choice to parents, professional responses which accept the parents' role in assessing or defining problems and support for both parents and professionals in creating new working relationships. Evidence from other areas such as health and education would suggest that progress is likely to be slow.

Use of the term partnership as a *mantra*, operating to support change that had already been achieved, is likely only to further entrench the view that partnership does not require change by professionals, and to reduce the confidence of clients and the community in social service provision. Even without substantial new resources it is possible to embark on the process of ceding power by sharing information and being open with clients, although social workers cannot be expected to do this without supportive policies and management. Parents cannot be expected to engage in the assessment of their child's needs or social services planning if their views are not taken seriously. It will, of course, not always be possible to do what parents want, but every departure from their wishes should be negotiated and fully explained. Understanding parents' reasons can provide a better basis for an agreed solution and help parents to orient their views in terms of their children's needs. Parents need to know more than this 'cannot be done' or that 'is not appropriate'. Work towards partnership with parents is likely to be more successful if it includes talking about the activity that one is engaged in, assessment, negotiation of an agreement, planning and focusing on parents' participation rather than merely labelling everything as 'working in partnership' and assuming that all its constituent elements have been addressed.

Notes

1. *Hounslow LBC v A* [1993] 1 F.L.R. 702, 708.
2. *R v North West Thames Regional Health Authority ex parte Daniels*, The Times, (22 July 1993).
3. *Re O (a minor) (medical treatment)* [1993] 1 F.L.R. 149.
4. Education Committee 3rd Report, *Meeting Special Educational Needs, Statements of Needs and Provision* (1992-3 H.C.P. 287, para. 16).
5. Education, Science and Arts Committee 3rd Report, *Special Educational Needs – Implementation of the Education Act 1982* (1986-7 H.C.P. 201).
6. Review of Children's Cases Regulations 1991 S.I. 898.
7. 1991 S.I. 890 reg. 3(4)(5).
8. *Re B (care: contact, local authority's plans)* [1993] 1 FLR 543 C.A. at p.551: 'The proposals of the local authority... must command the greatest respect and consultation from the court' (per Butler-Sloss L J).
9. Access to records is covered by the Access to Personal Files Act 1987. Guidance has been issued (LAC (88)17) which advised that disclosure for social work purposes can be made without the consent of the subject to people outside the social services department. (para. 18).
10. Housing Act 1985 (part III). Consideration is currently being given to reducing this duty.
11. *R v Tower Hamlets LBC ex parte Khatun*, The Independent, (30 September, 1993).
12. D.O.E./DoH/Welsh Office, 1991, Homeless Code of Guidance for Local Authorities (3rd ed.) para.6.16.
13. *R v Tower Hamlets L.B.C. ex parte Byas* (1992) 25 H.L.R. 105.
14. Education Act 1993, ss. 157, 169, 170.

3 Partnership between parents

Christine Piper

The title of this chapter is not unfinished: it focuses on the parents themselves rather than the partnership between parents and A.N.Other which is the theme of most chapters in this book. They illustrate that 'partnership under the Children Act 1989' is usually taken to mean partnership in relation to the statutory rights and duties arising out of the public law provisions in the Act, notably those contained in Parts III and IV where services for children in need and care and supervision are discussed. More widely 'partnership' is used as an ideal that emerged in practice and policy documents of the 1980s (see Masson pp.21-6) but still referring either to the partnership between parents and personnel in local authority departments, voluntary bodies and the medical and legal professions or to partnership between such personnel. There is also discussion of partnership between children and these professionals (DoH, 1991e and, very occasionally, there are references to 'parents working in partnership with other parents in self help groups' (Buchanan, 1993:6).

However, another partnership is envisaged by the *Children Act 1989*: that between parents given responsibility in relation to the same child by the private law provisions of the Act.[1] Whilst the nature of this legal relationship has been the subject of academic discussion,[2] what are usually ignored are its effects on the composition of the parental 'side' of the various partnerships that are promoted by the Act. A focus on the relationship between parents which results from the provisions of Parts I and II of the Act is not, therefore, out of place in a book which is primarily about the public law provisions. Furthermore, assumptions about the nature of this parental relationship underlie legal provisions, policy statements and professional practice and, therefore, affect the operation of partnership in regard to the care, education and protection of children.

The most important change in the private law introduced by the Act is the new legal concept of parental responsibility; what Kaganas has referred to as 'the lynchpin of the partnership ideology' (p.8). Its definition in section 3(1) of the Act is very broad: 'all the rights, duties, powers, responsibilities and authority which by law a parent of a child has in relation to the child and his property'. It gives married parents, and unmarried parents when the father has acquired parental responsibility by consent of the mother[3] or by a court order,[4] equality in terms of parental rights and authority, an equality which persists after divorce or separation. The continuing nature of this new concept opened up a range of different legal possibilities regarding the care and control of children which were seen as answers to problems outlined in the 1980s. In the area of private law the most pressing of these problems was caused by the increase in the incidence of divorce and the resulting need for the courts to make decisions about the custody of, and access to, a far larger number of children.[5] This produced practical and financial difficulties for busy courts[6] and led to judicial unease[7] that decisions about the welfare of the child were often being made in a routine way with insufficient information (Davis, Macleod and Murch 1983).

At the same time the Law Commission (1988:para.4.5), in its review of guardianship and custody of children, endorsed the principle that court orders should reduce the opportunities for conflict in the future: sole custody to one parent (usually the mother) and access to the other parent encouraged 'symbolic' litigation[8] and left out the father to the detriment of the child. Joint legal custody had been advocated as an answer to this dilemma by, for example, the Report of the Matrimonial Causes Procedure Committee (1985), but both this Committee and an earlier Law Commission Report (1986:para.4.41) warned against imposing joint custody on parents. Feminist academics in particular argued strongly that joint custody disadvantaged the mother and, by providing the non-caretaker with legal powers to intervene in decisions about the upbringing of the child, could lead to increased litigation.[9]

The Children Act 'solved' this dilemma by abolishing the legal concept of custody and, instead, gave the courts power, in section 8, to make four different orders: contact and residence (which include elements of the former access and custody orders) and specific issue and prohibited steps orders designed to give the opportunity for court adjudication of disputes in relation to parenting.[10] Taking the 'no order presumption' into account, the legislation apparently encourages private ordering on divorce and establishes a norm that parents remain 'jointly responsible' for their children after divorce. It has been argued that this is joint custody in all but name (Dewar, 1992; Kaganas and Piper, 1994). The presumption is that parents, given encouragement, would be able to negotiate how, jointly, to use their parental responsibility.

In other words the Children Act presupposed a form of 'co-operative relationship' which had been strongly advocated throughout the 1980s by child welfare practitioners. Research evidence supporting the benefits for children of cooperative parenting had accumulated since the 1970s[11] and had been used by mediators, legislators, mental health and child protection professionals and the judiciary to push for resources and procedural change to promote new ways of encouraging parental harmony, notably relating to the diminution of conflict when parents separate. In various jurisdictions mediators, marriage guidance counsellors and the judiciary have, therefore, organised or supported the establishment of programmes to 'educate' parents about divorce and the needs of children,[12] particularly their need for parents who are not in conflict, and also of procedures (for example, in-court mediation) which encourage settlement of parental disputes by parents. There is considerable pressure to persuade parents to be cooperative, especially in relation to attendance at, and the outcome of, mediation. For example, a recent article by a district judge on in-court mediation is sub-titled 'Head Banging' (Gerlis, 1994), an apparently common term to describe the efforts of professionals ('banging the parties' heads together') in relation to those parents who are perceived as being stubbornly resistant to making an agreement. Indeed, the Consultation Paper on divorce issued by the Lord Chancellor's Department (1993:para.9.22) suggests that public funding for divorce might be withheld if parents were unwilling to attend mediation.[13] The process of mediation also exerts pressure on parents. Davis and Bader quote a mother in their study of in-court mediation who told them,

> I don't see that a lot of good comes out of mediation – you are left with tremendous guilt if you haven't done enough yourself ... You're under tremendous pressure of time and tremendous pressure to reach a decision ... And because you're given the impression that it's *your* decision you have to live with your guilt (1985:44).

Nearly all the parents in my sample of parents attending out-of-court mediation also experienced both 'carrot' and 'stick' interventions to persuade them to agree (1993:131-144). Central to this process of 'manufacturing motivation' in parents, but also central to the process of defining the problem and selecting a solution in mediation, is the construction of a particular concept of parental responsibility, in which past patterns of parenting and parental expertise become irrelevant. If parents accept a construction of themselves as jointly responsible for the problem situation, the solution becomes a form of joint parenting which entails giving priority to communication and cooperation above care-taking (Piper, 1988).

It is clear from studies of mediation, therefore, that there are particular ideas about what joint parental responsibility, the parental partnership, 'means' and that these pre-date the Children Act 1989. These ideas have been given strong support by the legal concept of parental responsibility which stresses the decision-making component of responsibility: the role of law is confined to adjudicating when parents cannot make an agreed decision, whether about residence, contact or the other 'major' issues which form part of the reported cases on prohibited steps and specific issues orders.

Why is a particular idea about the nature of parental partnership so prevalent and so powerful? The notion of a continuing parental responsibility is not new in legal or social discourses but its recent incorporation into statute raises questions about the nature of law. Law can set out forms of behaviour which act as ideals to be striven for or which are a symbol of the power of the group responsible for its passage.[14] Concepts which are politically and morally charged may be introduced into legislation to reinforce them so that particular ideas become politically coherent. This, according to Edwards and Halpern (1992), is what the parental responsibility provisions have achieved. They argue that the Child Support Act 1991 and the Criminal Justice Act 1991 as well as the Children Act 1989 have all used a concept of parental responsibility as an instrument of social policy (see also Kaganas at p.8) to give a clear moral message that 'parenting is for life'[15] and to encourage the belief that parents (rather than, for example, social and economic policies) are responsible for juvenile delinquency, family poverty and the standard of education. This circular process has strengthened the myth that there is a 'parenting unit', based, at least as a starting point, on a traditional nuclear family of two parents and their child(ren)[16] and in which there exists, or could exist, parental cooperation and negotiation.

The Act, however, does not provide any mechanisms for such cooperation between parents: there is no legal pressure on those with parental responsibility to consult each other (Bainham, 1990a:192).[17] As Hadfield and Lavery point out, in contrast with the mandatory consultation in which local authorities must engage when acting in partnership with parents and children,

> The law does not require one parent to take into account the view of the other, when reaching a decision in relation to their child. Each parent with parental responsibility can act alone and without the other, unless statutes require the consent of more than one person in the matter (1991:466).[18]

Because of this omission, Bainham argues that,

> The conclusion must surely be that the dual objectives of promoting agreements and providing for parental independence were considered to reflect the public interest in children better than the assertion of a partnership between parents based on co-operative decision-making (1990c:213).

The Children Act 1989, whilst assuming the existence of some form of parental partnership has not provided the legal nuts and bolts – for example, presumptions about consultation – for such a partnership. Whether, therefore, it has encouraged, or reinforced more 'joint' parenting is doubtful: there is evidence that parenting generally is not joint in any real sense. A review of research in Sweden and the USA led to the comment that the division of labour in relation to housework and child care 'does not come close to parity' (Calasanti and Bailey, 1991:49) and small scale research in the UK supports this assertion (see Piper, 1993:161-5; Clulow and Vincent, 1987:112-4). Neither does research show an increase in shared child care after divorce. A review of research projects undertaken by the Centre for Policy Research in Denver, Colorado since 1981 concludes, 'We have found that the joint custody label alone does not make parents equal partners in child-rearing' (Pearson, 1993:297).

Decision-making

Even less is known about parental decision-making on matters relating to their children despite a large literature on child care and marital role segregation. In addition, research in the area of family decision-making is particularly fraught with methodological and conceptual difficulties.[19] What evidence there is does not suggest that, either before or after separation, parental decision-making is usually a negotiated process.[20] A review of research in the USA in the 1980s supports the conclusion that few parents in 'intact' families engage in decision-making which is not either an 'assumed' agreement or an imposed outcome (Thompson and Walker, 1989).

Again, small scale studies in the UK confirm this. Edgell (1980), for example, interviewed a sample of middle class mothers and fathers separately to construct a hierarchy of decisions in terms of their perceived importance. He found that, whilst the majority of husbands and wives reported that decisions were made jointly in half the decisions, nearly all the 'very important' and infrequent decisions were made by the husband alone and the 'not important' and frequent decisions tended to be left to the wife. So, in regard to the two types of parenting decisions discussed, the children's education was decided jointly and considered to be a very important area whereas decisions about children's clothes were made by the wife alone and considered frequent and unimportant (1980:58). My study included discussions with sixteen fathers and fourteen mothers (who had recently experienced divorce medi-ation) about thirteen decision areas concerned with child-rearing. Almost 40 percent of the 266 parent-answers this exercise yielded were 'jointly decided', only 4.5 percent were 'father only' and 54 percent were 'mother only'. These results are not indicative of widespread joint decision-making given that they cannot be explained by mothers 'voting for themselves' and that the 'jointly

decided' category was dominated by answers to two decisions –
where children were to be born and whether children should be
involved in any religious activity or instruction – where the
outcome had usually been determined, respectively, by medical
advice and by default (Piper, 1993:41-9).

After separation parents may well, therefore, be encouraged to
engage in an entirely novel experience of negotiating settlement of
their dispute. A recently completed study of divorced parents in the
USA by Maccoby and Mnookin found that parental discussions
were confined to a small range of child-related issues and that joint
decisions were made only in a small minority of their sample (1992:
Tables 9.5 and 9.6). There is no comparable study in the UK but one
indicator of parental cooperation or conflict after divorce might be
the amount of legal activity engaged in by parents. If so, in the UK,
if legal changes had led to more, not less, conflict, one would expect
a high number of applications for specific issue and prohibited
steps orders; those orders available to the courts if parents bring
disputes over parenting issues. However, statistics for the first two
years of the Children Act's operation show relatively small numbers
of applications for these orders. For example, prohibited steps
applications peaked at 2611 in the third quarter of 1992 and were
down to 1262 in the fourth quarter of 1993.[21] There has been a large
increase in the number of contact applications though it is possible
this trend was temporary.[22] Reported decisions of the Family
Division and the Appeal Court do not reveal any increase in the
number or scope of parental disputes coming before the courts with
only 21 reported private law cases in over two and a half years
where a prohibited steps or specific order was the issue.[23] Yet there
are reasons not to count this as evidence. The pressure to divert
parental disputes to mediation, the Legal Aid rules[24] and the no
order presumption would suggest that legal advisors would not
encourage the use of litigation.

Despite the increased emphasis on the importance of parenting
and assumptions of 'shared' parenting there is, therefore, no
conclusive evidence to support the existence of widespread joint
parenting either before or after parents separate. This has several
potential implications in terms of parental rights and needs as well
as the welfare of the child in relation to the provision of services for,
and protection of, children. First, an assumption that there is a
parental partnership involving shared care, in whatever proportions, encourages the belief that both parents have experience in
assessing and meeting their child's needs. Professionals who might
have responded by providing help and supervision cannot do so if
they are 'blind' to the possibility that one parent in the partnership
does not have such experience. In mediation, for example, solutions
may be discussed without reference to the inexperience or even
incompetency of one parent (Piper, 1993:113-4). There will also be
no policies to redress resource deficiencies which are hidden by the

assumption that a partnership is in operation.[25]

Secondly, the prevalent blindness to the possibility that a 'parental partnership' between two or more people with parental responsibility may not in fact exist has administrative consequences. Suitable procedures and practices may not be developed to respond to those situations where 'the parents' in partnership with others as encouraged by the Act are not a unit but individuals either in conflict or not in contact.

Thirdly, the use of the 'neutral' term 'parents' renders invisible gender issues and may lead to insufficient acknowledgement that the parental 'unit' may be more or less than two parents. In all these instances the needs of particular mothers, fathers and significant others may not be met.

Partnership in education

As yet there has been comparatively little written on these issues in relation to the Children Act 1989. However, education law and practice, where forms of statutory and voluntary partnership have been developing over more than a decade, constitute an area which very clearly reveals the practical difficulties and the discrimination which can arise when professional practice assumes parents are in partnership.[26] Throughout the 1980s there were two trends in relation to parents. First, the growing political emphasis on parent choice in education led to the provision of various statutory rights for parents to be involved in decision-making on educational matters, ranging from the right to be involved in a ballot regarding an application for grant maintained status[27] to the right to be involved in the choice of school.[28] These rights have created a partnership of parents and the local education authority or school governors in the making of certain key decisions. Secondly, there was increasing practical involvement of parents in the school (including the classroom itself) which entailed a partnership between teachers and parents in the provision of education.[29]

The Children Act is relevant to the first trend because it altered the definition of parent in relation to the Education Acts. The previous statutory definition of 'parent' in this context was provided by the Education Act 1944, whereby a parent included 'a guardian and any person who has the actual custody of the child or young person'. The Children Act in s114(1D) added a new definition which states that a 'parent' now 'includes any person who is not a parent ... but who has parental responsibility ... or care of a child'.[30] This means that those who have acquired parental responsibility now count as 'parents' for education purposes and that those who are given parental responsibility for the duration of their child's childhood also retain their educational 'rights' during that period. As has been pointed out 'Partnership requires

informed participation' (DoH, 1991e:para.2-28): parents need
relevant information to make choices about education. Education
authorities and schools must either 'publish' such information (for
example, the school prospectus and comparative tables of examination results and truancy rates)[31] or make it available to parents (for
example, annual reports of the child's achievements).[32] If the child
has two parents who are living together they will normally jointly
receive the necessary information via their child or the post.

These methods of conveying information to the child's home,
together with an assumption that any response to such information
will be jointly made, are satisfactory if there is a parental unit and
there are two parents who are of one mind or who can negotiate
disagreement. Certainly education legislation does not provide for
situations where this is not so. The 1980 Education Act imposes a
duty on the LEA (or governors of other schools) 'to comply with any
preference expressed by a parent in regard to the school at which he
wishes education to be provided for his child'.[33] The statutory
exceptions to this duty do not provide for a situation involving
conflicting preferences by parents.[34] This is a serious omission in
view of the fact that parents are not always in agreement about
educational decisions even when living together. Miriam David
provides evidence of disagreement: she cites the small scale
research study of Elliot et al. (1981) who found that mothers and
fathers had different criteria for choice of school and studies by Fox
(1985) and Johnson (1987) which found that mothers and fathers
had different reasons and preferred outcomes in relation to the
choice of private or state education.[35] In this situation of the intact
family parents are likely to reach agreement or, failing that, one
parent's views prevail over the other.

But the situation is more complicated if there is an 'absent' father.
Divorced fathers, irrespective of their involvement in the upbringing of their child(ren), retain parental responsibility and
parental responsibility orders have been made by courts in favour
of an unmarried father 'even where there is little or no prospect of
the father having contact with the child' (Butler et al. 1993:157). It is
theoretically possible, therefore, that a parent with little experience
of the child's needs and preferences and who has no experience of
parenting jointly with the care-taking parent may legally exercise
his rights in regard to his child's education without the knowledge
or consent of the other parent. Furthermore, the situation may be
made more complex by the existence of other persons with parental
responsibility, for example a grandparent, step-parent or foster
parent. As yet, guidance from the Department for Education (DFE)
has not fully grasped the implications of this[36] but guidance
produced by the Open University for use by the DFE includes the
following statement:

> All those with parental responsibility must be treated equally by schools
> and LEA staff ... All are entitled, for instance, to vote in elections for

Parent Governors, or in ballots concerning the school's status, and to participate in assessments for special educational needs. All are entitled to receive school reports **if they request them** (1991:10) (my emphasis).

This would seem to acknowledge the existence of a right to equal treatment by all defined as parents though the problems which result from such a right are addressed only in regard to the issue of school reports and the solution discriminates between persons with responsibility in that at least one parent with responsibility (or care of the child) will acquire the report without so requesting, the other(s) will not. Ben Whitney has referred to the 'failure by many schools to make all reasonable efforts to ensure that such rights and opportunities are offered without favour ... many schools are depriving parents of their rights ... by not making sufficient efforts to identify them as 'registered parents' ' (Whitney, 1994). Parents who do not know when or how to ensure their inclusion on the relevant documentation at their children's schools or how to obtain information will not be part of the parental partnership in decision-making on education issues. This makes life simpler for the local authority or school in that conflicting preferences are less likely to arise if only one parent is given the opportunity to acquire information and record decisions. If schools do make greater efforts to involve all 'parents' then the lack of procedures for dealing with conflicting preferences will have to be remedied. In other words, the absence of partnership in practice between parents has important ramifications for partnership with schools. The current situation may make life simpler for the care-taking parent as well as the school but, as we shall see occurs in relation to the second trend, may impose a burden in that the 'weight' of the partnership falls on one parent only

Gender issues

The second partnership trend in education – that of the practical involvement of a parent with a school – was an idea copied from the USA in the 1960s which focused first on nursery and first school education and was publicised in the UK in the Plowden Report (Central Advisory Council for Education, 1967). A review of research written in 1983 said that the most popular forms of parental participation in schools were: helping on school visits and outings, sewing and cooking and doing minor repairs to equipment as well as listening to children reading and helping with number work and specific projects. In several areas parents also participated in schemes in which they were asked to hear their children read regularly at home (Pugh, 1983:1). Such policies,

relied upon the notion of 'maternal' availability to aid or learn about their children's schooling (David, 1985). The concept of parent education, despite its gender-neutral terminology, required mothers' involvement in the daily activities of schools (David, 1991:438).

For example, in some schools, there are clear expectations that mothers will regularly be involved in teaching their child(ren) the 3Rs (David, 1993; Ch 8). Yet the greater practical involvement of mothers rather than fathers has not been acknowledged. In a chapter entitled *Mothers in Education or Mum's the Word?* Miriam David argues, 'Despite the fact that there has been an enormous amount of research evidence about different aspects of the parents' role in education ... little of it has differentiated between fathers and mothers' (David, 1993:158) – a contention easily substantiated by a trawl along library shelves.[37] Bastiani, for instance, in his critique of partnership in education (1993), draws attention to the 'huge discrepancy between the common usage [of the term 'partnership'] and any careful consideration of its meanings' (1993:104) and yet gender is not mentioned in his discussion of educational practice in regard to partnership. Similarly, in a very prescriptive book, *Schools and Parents*, Partington and Wragg never discuss parents as mothers and fathers even in the 'learning to read' section (1989:62).

Because the often greater involvement of women has been invisible, educational policy, as David points out, has not taken into account those changes in the 1980s in family forms relating to the role of women (1991a:439-41). The increase in the number of families headed by a lone parent and female employment patterns in particular have made this involvement more difficult at a time when increasing normative pressure to encourage involvement is evident in the pronouncements of politicians and the publications of the DFE. For example, Kenneth Baker (former Education Secretary) in the 1987 Churchill Lecture said, 'Teaching is a difficult enough task made even more difficult when parents don't take their responsibilities seriously enough.'[38] The Parent's Charter gave the same message: 'You owe it to your child to find time and room for such activities if you can and to attend meetings and other events at the school' (DES, 1991 p.19). *Our Children's Education*, the up-dated version of the Charter (DFE, 1994), in the section subtitled 'Partnership in Education' begins 'The Charter will help you get the best education for your child. You can do this most successfully as an active partner with the school and its teachers' (1994:25) and later suggests, 'You might like to share your skills and interests with pupils and teachers and attend outings and other events at the school' (1994:26).

Given that the decision-making partnership may also be dependent for its operation on a considerable investment of time and energy in gaining the relevant information, what is conveyed in political rhetoric as 'parent power' may be perceived as unwanted responsibility falling on only one parent. As a result, the frequent experience of partnership between parents and schools may be perceived as an extra care-taking 'chore'. It may also be seen as a form of 'education' of parents which applies unequally. As Pugh commented a decade ago 'many schools appear to be attempting ... to change parents' behaviour rather than trying to establish a dialogue with parents' (1983:2). In other words, partnership may entail a form of social control of parents which in practice controls mainly mothers.

There is also evidence of the unequal burdens that arise in relation to one form of pre-school education: that of playgroups. Recent research on their management is relevant not only because the playgroup movement was an important site 'for the development of the idea of partnership between parents and workers in the voluntary sector' but also because a DES Report (1990) setting out objectives for nursery education argued that they could only be achieved within a staff-parents partnership model (Brophy, 1994: 161-6).[39] Based on playgroups in a rural local authority and an inner city borough, Julia Brophy's research found that those parents who became managers of playgroups were mothers 'mostly drawn from white, higher income higher educational groups with a clear under-representation of particular groups of parents, especially working class mothers, black and minority ethnic mothers and all categories of fathers' (1994:191). Like David she argues that using the terminology of 'parents' and 'users' 'serves to obscure certain issues' but extends her concern to the issues of race and class as well as gender which are masked by the concept of partnership. She points out, however, that those who are involved in partnership in playgroups do not necessarily feel they are privileged to do so or empowered by the experience: 31 percent of rural and 42 percent of inner city mother-managers had mixed or negative views about being a manager (1994: Table 4). Scott's sample of mothers in Strathclyde also revealed 'considerable ambivalence' about such parental participation (Scott, 1990).[40] In both samples mothers felt that involvement in partnership imposed extra 'mothering' burdens with or without compensating benefits.

Implications for practice

This brief discussion of how partnership between parent and teacher, playgroup leader, school and education authority operates in practice and is affected by the partnership, or lack of it, between parents, reveals issues of concern for partnership between and with parents which might also be applicable to various forms of partnership under the Children Act 1989. First, professionals, enjoined to work in partnership with parents in those situations where they must consult parents and share, or defer to, the parental responsibility accorded to certain parents and others, cannot assume that one parent speaks for another. They may also need to devise procedures which take into account that what a child refers to as her 'family' may cover a variety of situations in which one or more parents feature and in which one of these parents may not have parental responsibility whilst a non-parent does. The very real possibility that in different situations of partnership under the Children Act a person legally entitled to be part of the 'parent' half of a partnership is not in practice part of that partnership needs addressing. Such a person may either be disadvantaged or spared a burden because of their omission but the proper implementation of the law as well as the welfare of the child requires that such an omission should not result merely from administrative muddle or bad practice. The Children Act does not say that partnership should be practised only with those 'parents' most readily available and, perhaps, most easily managed. Harrison and Masson have argued that social workers, if trying to work in partnership with all parents, ought to counter those 'ideological commitments which have led them to marginalise and attenuate the role of parents and other significant people in the child's life' (1994:42).[41]

Secondly, professional practice may not take into account that 'parents' are mothers or fathers with different roles, resources and expectations. If the parental unit is viewed in terms which do not specify gender, then sexist practice may not be addressed. Judith Milner's research into child protection practices provides evidence that sexist practice exists (Milner, 1993) and Ward and Mullender draw attention to the fact that, despite attempts in the 1980s to conceptualise gender-informed social work practices, a feminist perspective is still little more than a veneer or an added extra to social work theory and practice (1990/2:25)[42] Women are seen as responsible for their children and so blamed for inadequacy and negligence when something goes wrong, even though children are more likely to die at the hands of male carers.[43] 'This means that the term parenting, though an attempt at gender neutrality, is nothing but an empty gesture. Fathering, being ill-defined yet of higher status than mothering, is inaccessible to scrutiny in child protection terms' (Milner, 1993:52). She explains this as a combination of two factors. First, there is an understandable reluctance to confront 'on their own doorsteps (a man's home is his castle)' (1994:53) men who have experienced no scrutiny of their role as father (unlike mothers who have been 'screened' through pregnancy and early parent-hood) and who may be known to be violent. Secondly, there is a lack of adequate social work techniques and knowledge base to cope with such fathers (1994:55). There is also a concentration on the mother because of an assumption, supported in relation to sexual abuse, by 'a long tradition in the literature of accusing women of collusion in the incest' which has only recently been challenged by feminist scholars (DeYoung, 1994:81), that she could control the abuse inflicted by the father. Waterhouse and Carnie found, for example, in their Scottish study of 51 cases of familial sexual abuse dealt with in 1987 (in which all but one of the perpetrators were men) that the attitude of the non-abusing parent to the alleged perpetrator 'more than any other criterion' was seen as 'the litmus test of the children's likely safety' (1992:51).

So strong is institutional and practice bias towards a focus on mothers that Milner, though theoretically well aware of gender issues, found (during a six month period of practice in a child protection team) that she 'had unconsciously operated all the filters which serve to legitimate male authority over women' (1993:57) and that, in her own case load, when the allegation had been against the father only, there was no action taken after investigation whilst in investigations leading to full case conferences 'it was the presence of a possibly negligent or stressed mother which was the major factor' (1993:58). Such a procedure may increase the chances of the mother's access to resources but 'carries with it the danger of underestimating the effects of their unhelpful partners' (1993:59). She therefore suggests a list of seven practical suggestions for improving matters including a proposal that 'fathers' be explicitly included on forms (1993:60).

Furthermore, when social work literature acknowledges gender it does not necessarily mean that social work practice will take into account the needs and problems specific to mothers. Braun, for instance, asks workers not to assume that 'parent means mother' but goes on to argue for practice which leads to the involvement of other carers such as fathers and grandparents without addressing the needs of the parent carrying the major burden (1992; 178). A review of US literature on lone fathers, aimed explicitly at providing information that 'will aid social work practice with lone fathers in Great Britain' (Greif, 1992:565) points to 'problems' which such fathers have that need addressing. 'When a father cannot pursue a job as he could have when his wife was in the home, his self-esteem may suffer' (Greif, 1992:572). There are many mothers who have felt such loss of self-esteem! Marian Brandon, in referring to a small case study carried out in 1991, discussed cases where the fact that mothers' needs were not acknowledged at the outset had made working in partnership a difficult and protracted process (1992:25). She also noted that the requirements of 'reasonable parenting' in relation to mothers 'also seemed to be more stringent than for fathers' (1992:28).

It is not only child protection services which consider the mother to be the focus of their partnership even when there is a father on hand. Jo Van Every provides evidence of such practice by health workers (1991/2:68-9). One example from her own research is of a heterosexual couple who shared child care. The father was looking after the baby at the time of the visit from the health visitor and, when both parents were working, it was the nanny who took the baby to the clinic; in both instances it was made clear that the mother should have been present (1991/2:68).

One may validly argue, therefore, that partnership, rather than being a mechanism for the empowerment of parents, may be another vehicle for the 'regulation' of women. Carol-Ann Hooper contrasts such regulation in two historical periods: 1870-1930 when the focus was the behaviour of sexually abused girls themselves (though often in the name of their future as mothers) and the period from the 1970s to the present when the behaviour of mothers of sexually abused children has been the prime concern of the child protection agencies (1992:52-3). She contends that, despite policy shifts in regard to the balance between state intervention and family autonomy, child care work has always focused on mothers. She looks at those knowledge bases used by social workers which have legitimated the increased 'surveillance' of women as mothers of sexually abused children (1992:68). Family dysfunction theory (part of the medical discourse) has been drawn on to attribute fault to the mother (who might then internalise such blame) and has, therefore, been the focus of a feminist critique. However, she considers that the child protection discourse, though not concerned with causality, has been more influential because it constructs the mother as the key person in preventing further abuse and therefore accords her sole responsibility for the child's welfare. This could empower mothers, by giving them entitlements to priority help for example, but she points out that the women in her study who approached agencies for help when their children were abused 'sometimes received little but surveillance of themselves in return' (1992:72). Therefore, just as Masson has argued for the 'disaggregation' of partnership into its component parts in various contexts (pp.27-8) Hooper argues for the disaggregation of parents so that the parents are not perceived automatically as a partnership – 'an indivisible unit with identical interests obscuring the conflicts between them' – and the social work tendency to accord to mothers 'greater power than they had to control abusive men' is undermined (1992:72).

The debate on these issues, though often ignored, is currently of practical importance. The recent CCETSW Paper (1991) on the rules and requirements for the Diploma in Social Work has led to the development of diploma programmes with a strong emphasis on anti-discriminatory practice. Hooper also refers to the change in thinking revealed in Department of Health guidelines for social workers (1992:75). For example, it no longer explains incestuous abuse by reference to 'distorted family relationships' (DHSS, 1988). Moira Kirwan, believing that 'it might be reasonable to expect that social work training is now going to take on board the issue of gender' (1994:137) has studied the eighteen new diploma programmes running in Scotland in 1991-2. On the basis of that research, looking at syllabuses and talking to those involved in relation to five criteria for gender awareness in training, she argues that pressure has led to a focus on practice issues in relation to gender but that gender 'oppression' within the social work profession itself has not been tackled. The thrust of her article is that the two forms of oppression are interlinked and that 'unless the connection is made and becomes a central part of social work training, there will be no real change and women workers will continue to assist in their own oppression by oppressing women clients' (Kirwan, 1994:139).

I hope this is a pessimistic view. Feminists promoting 'parenting' in order to stress that mothers do not have to do the 'mothering' are again caught in the dilemma that such a strategy is counter productive as long as most mothers continue to bear an inequitable burden within the parenting partnership. 'Parents' do need to be visible again as mothers and fathers and others. There needs to be a discussion of the problems and needs of each component (or sole component) of the parental partnership. This would make clear that the parent/professional partnership is usually a mother/professional partnership which imposes unacknowledged burdens on women. This might then lead to a better deal for mothers. It might also lead to a different role for fathers, in relation to partnership and parenting, in those families where the father's involvement in parenting is more than nominal. The report of a study by Herbert and Carpenter of seven fathers with Down's Syndrome babies reveals enormous grief made worse by the actions of professionals who, focusing solely on the mother and child, 'left out' the father who then found difficulty in constructing a useful parenting role in so far as work constraints permitted. In the language of the 1990s they argue that 'services should be tailored to meet individual consumer needs not pre-packaged' (Herbert and Carpenter, 1994: 40). The current paradox in assumptions about the partnership between parents makes achieving this aim difficult. Where there is a father living in the family, partnership is assumed: fathers have to do very little, if anything, in such circumstances to qualify as partners. Because of this assumption the professional response rarely includes attempts to seek out and remedy a lack of partnership in ways which advantage the mother. Yet, a professional response which focuses on the mother is implicitly based on an assumption that there is no partnership and that the mother has sole influence over the welfare of the child: an assumption that is sometimes but not always true. Until the implications of the relationship set up between parents by the Children Act 1989 are examined in conjunction with those stemming from the parent/ state relationships set up by that Act there is little chance of real partnership in either sense.

Notes

1. This is not usually discussed, however, in terms of 'partnership under the Act'. Jane Aldgate does put this as the first in a 'four-fold partnership' to achieve the aim of the promotion of the welfare of children under the Children Act 1989 though she confines its scope to those parents who are living apart and its aim to ensuring 'the safe unbringing of their children' (Aldgate, 1991:5).
2. See, for example, Bainham (1990a); Eekelaar (1991) and Roche (1991).
3. Section 4(1)(b).
4. Section 4(1)(a). Parental responsibility can also be acquired by obtaining a residence order (but only for the duration of the residence order) under section 12(1) and by being appointed guardian under section 5(1-6).
5. In 1954 there were approximately 20,000 children under 16 whose parents obtained divorces (McGregor, 1957:5). This compares with over 160,000 thirty years later: see Piper (1993:7).
6. Section 41 of the Matrimonial Causes Act (since amended by Schedule 2, para. 31 of the Children Act 1989) imposed a duty on judges and registrars not to make a decree nisi absolute unless they stated in court that they were satisfied with the proposed arrangements for the children.
7. Sir Riger Ormrod, for example, expressed concern that judges were expected to have 'that old fashioned and often forgotten quality which used to be called wisdom' in order to make such decisions when 'conventional moral values are no longer acceptable as "guidelines" and the conclusions of the social sciences are at best unstable' (6th Hilda Lewis Memorial Lecture, quoted in Murch, 1980:213).
8. See, King (1987).
9. See, for example, Brophy and Smart (eds) (1985); Smith (1984) and Fineman (1991).
10. There is technically a fifth section 8 order: that to discharge a section 8 order. See Smith (1993).
11. For a brief review of some of this literature see Piper (1994a).
12. See Petersen and Steinman (1994) and Lehner (1994) for descriptions of two mandatory programmes of 'education' operating in the USA. In the UK the recent Consultation Paper issued by the Lord Chancellor's Department (1993) proposes an 'initial interview' which would include giving parents advice and information about the process of divorce and the welfare of children.
13. Paragraph 9.8 of the Consultation Document (Lord Chancellor's Department, 1993) states that 'it would be a condition of publicly funded assistance that those receiving it should behave reasonably in all the circumstances' and in para. 9.22 an example of behaving unreasonably is given – 'where he or she refuses even to contemplate mediation'.
14. Such 'symbolic legislation' may entrench the interests of those in power or it may symbolise a past and waning power: see Gusfield's study of the temperance legislation in the USA (Gusfield, 1973).
15. A phrase used by the then Prime Minister, Mrs Thatcher. See the discussion by Gillian Douglas (1990).
16. See, for example, Van Every (1991/2).
17. However, see *Re G (a Minor)* (5 Jan 1993) where Glidewell, L. J. stated that a non-caretaking mother was entitled to be consulted about the child's schooling.
18. See the Children Act section 2(7).
19. See Piper (1993:38-41) for a review of the literature.
20. See Piper (1993:137) for a discussion of the five possible models to describe the process of parental decision-making.
21. Statistics kindly supplied by the Information Management Unit of the Lord Chancellor's Department in January 1994.

22. See the Children Act Advisory Committee's Annual Reports for 1991/2 and 1992/3.
23. A further 23 cases included references by the judge to these orders or applications for them in the history of the case. See Kaganas and Piper (1994) for a discussion of cases reported in the first 21 months of the Act's operation. Cases reported since (up to April 1994) do not reveal any different trends (I am grateful to Felicity Kaganas for supplying the additional data).
24. Section 8 applications are subject to the usual means and merits tests but, in addition, the Legal Aid office must consider 'whether the court is likely to intervene and make an order at all given the non-intervention principle in s 1(5) of the Act' (Legal Aid Handbook 1992: para. 7.21).
25. In another context – that of pre-school playgroups – Janet Finch's research led her to a similar conclusion that self-help and partnership ideas are 'deceitful' in that they mask a covert agenda of encouraging women 'to take on more unpaid health and welfare work' which avoids the need for higher cost statutory help (Finch, 1984:17-8).
26. Although this is not relevant to the focus of this chapter, education also provides a useful case study in relation to the lack of partnership in practice between statutory bodies affected by provisions of the Act. For example, Whalley, referring to section 27 of the Children Act 1989 which he calls the 'basis for cooperation' between various local authority departments, comments, 'But it seemed no one expected this to happen' because of an assumption that the Children Act 'belonged to social services' (1993:5).
27. Education Reform Act 1988 sections 60-73.
28. Education Act 1980 sections 6-7. For discussion of these and other parental rights see, for example, Harris and Bijsterveld (1993:186-7); David (1993: chapter 6).
29. See David (1993: chapter 5) for a historical review of the development and justifications for parental involvement in education.
30. For a discussion see Harris (1992) and Advisory Centre for Education (1992).
31. Education (School Information) (England) Regulations 1993 S.I. No. 1502; Education (School Performance Information) (England) Regulations 1993 S.I. 1992 No. 1503.
32. Education Reform Act 1988 s22.
33. At sections 6(2) and 6(1) respectively.
34. The Children Act 1989, rather than the Education Acts, provides a mechanism for settling such disputes in the form of section 8 applications for specific issue or prohibited steps orders.
35. See David (1991a:441).
36. See Piper (1994:6-9).
37. See also David et al. (1993). Referring to politicians who have recently attacked 'woolly' educationalists Miller makes the same point about the invisibility of gender: 'They are, in fact, attacking a largely female work-force and traditions of research and practice which have in many cases been initiated and taken up by women professionals. But they do not say so: any more than they say who they mean by parents. For those parents who are most likely to be active as participants in their children's schooling ... are much more likely to be women than men, too' (Miller, 1992:7).
38. December 1987, Cambridge, quoted in the National Association of Head Teachers (1990) *The Home-School Contract of Partnership*.
39. See Pugh (1985) for a discussion of the benefits that partnership is seen to produce for children.
40. Discussed in David (1993:165-6).
41. Harrison and Masson (1994) suggest this is particularly relevant to the social work response to parents who have been 'lost' to those young people already in care before the Children Act 1989. Their research will lead to suggestions for good practice to re-establish links with lost parents.

42. See, for example, Hanmer and Statham (1988) for a feminist approach to social work practice.
43. See Parton, C. (1990).

4 Partnership: reflections on some Canadian experiences

Alison Diduck*

Canada, like the United Kingdom, wrestled in the 1980s with the task of reconceptualising the roles of family and state in caring for and protecting children from harm. The result in England and Wales was, of course, the Children Act 1989, with its dominant themes of parental responsibility, welfare, and partnership. In the common law jurisdictions of Canada as well, these themes can be teased out of the legislation of the 1980s, although Canadian understandings of these themes are sometimes slightly different from their English counterparts. Each provincial legislature in Canada has, nonetheless, made statutory provision for the establishment of agencies mandated to provide services for the care and protection of children. Unlike the Children Act 1989, however, these statutes deal only with the public aspect of child care law; when questions of private child care arise, for example, in the context of divorce, other statutes apply. It is only when the state most directly intervenes in the 'private' family relationship, then, that the statutory powers and responsibilities of child care agencies are invoked.

In many ways, the powers given to these child care agencies seem almost draconian in the context of a society increasingly influenced by a discourse of individual and civil rights which are protected by a constitutionally entrenched Charter of Rights and Freedoms.[1] Interestingly, however, infringements of the Charter's protection which would, in many other contexts, result in the relegation of the offending provision to the status of 'being of no force and effect', have consistently been upheld in the context of society's responsibility to protect children from harm. This conflation of principles can be seen in the 'Charter-proofing' of some post-1982 child protection statutes (Thompson, 1989b), contrasted with the surpris-

* The author is grateful for the research assistance and advice of Marlene Lagimodiere of Legal Aid Manitoba, who provided advice regarding recent child protection practice issues in Manitoba, and about the practice and procedures of Legal Aid Manitoba. Ms. Lagimodiere is, among other things, 'duty counsel' at the twice weekly child protection docket courts in Winnipeg, Manitoba, Canada.

ing and seemingly anti-civil libertarian provisions which remain in others. So, for example, while the Ontario Child and Family Services Act[2] stresses 'due process', non-intervention and family autonomy, the Manitoba Child and Family Services Act[3] includes these ideas[4] yet also retains relatively vague grounds for the removal of children from the home without warrant or court order (see Thompson 1989b). Section 21 of the Manitoba Act says that:

> the director, a representative of an agency or a peace officer who on reasonable and probable grounds believes that a child is in need of protection, may apprehend the child without a warrant and take the child to a place of safety....

Section 17 states that a child is in need of protection 'where the life, health or emotional well being of that child' is endangered by the 'act or omission of a person.'[5] The Manitoba Act further denies the parties (that is, the parents and the agency) the right of pre-trial discovery,[6] and allows agencies to compel and cross examine parents at trial[7] (see Thompson, 1989b:145). Each of these provisions, were they to be part of a criminal law regime, would almost certainly be found to violate Charter protection against vagueness, procedural unfairness and self-incrimination.

However, the statutes do not contain only draconian measures. Just as in the Children Act 1989, most provincial legislation acknowledges that drastic intervention, usually in the form of their compulsory removal from the home, known as 'apprehension' in Manitoba,[8] may not promote the welfare of children at all. Rather, preventative measures, in the form of the provision of services to families on a voluntary basis, are usually seen as a better way to promote the welfare of families and of individual children. In this regard, statutes tend to speak in terms of the 'best interests' of children, giving this concept a similar pre-eminence to its English counterpart, the 'welfare' of children.[9] Similarly, although the word 'partnership' is found nowhere in the legislation, the concept of families and agencies working together to achieve agreed-upon goals to promote the best interests of children is fundamental to most of the legislation in the country. These statutes provide for voluntary arrangements to be made between agencies and families, some of which involve voluntary agreements,[10] while others require agencies to provide services to be maintained for families in order to prevent the removal of children from their homes.[11]

It is this voluntary notion of partnership which is most directly a part of Canadian statutes. Unlike the Children Act 1989, under the Manitoba CFS Act, for example, once a child is 'apprehended', or taken into care, the apprehending agency is 'responsible for the child's care, maintenance, education and well being', and it may 'authorize the provision of medical or dental care... without the consent of the parent or guardian and without an order of the court.'[12] Similarly, if the need for protection is subsequently proved in court, and the court makes an order either for permanent or temporary guardianship of the child to the agency, the agency shall:

(a)   have the care and control of the child;
(b)   be responsible for the maintenance and education of the child;
(c)   act for and on behalf of the child; and
(d)   appear in any court and prosecute and defend any action or proceeding in which the child's status is or may be affected.[13]

Significantly, then, there is little attempt in Manitoba to promote principles of partnership after non-voluntary agency intervention. The only exception is with regard to parental access to the child, which I will discuss later, and which may not promote this notion of partnership at all, but, rather, provide evidence of ideological commitment to other principles entirely. Partnership between agency and parents, then, is most clearly encouraged in Manitoba at the early, voluntary stage of state involvement with families.

In Manitoba there are two types of child care agency which provide these voluntary services to families: 'mandated' and 'non-mandated' agencies. 'Mandated' agencies are authorised by statute to apprehend children they believe are in need of protection. 'Non-mandated' agencies are usually government funded but do not fall under the ambit of the CFS Act, and do not have the authority to apprehend. Both types of agencies, however, are able to offer a wide range of child and family support services, including home-makers, parent aides, counselling services and parenting skills courses. 'Mandated' agencies place 'home-makers' in a home with the agreement of the parent(s). Home-makers are authorised to enter and live in the home, use any equipment or apparatus in the home to carry on normal housekeeping activities as are necessary to care for the child properly, to exercise reasonable control and discipline over the child, and to provide training, teaching, and counselling to parents to assist them in properly caring for the child.[14] They are similar to the range of 'home visitors' in England who offer assistance to families with medical, educational, home-making, and parenting matters (David, 1991b: 109-112). 'Parent aides' are placed in a home with the consent of the parents to provide training in home-making and child care.[15] Each of these services is required to be provided by 'mandated' agencies pursuant to their statutory duties,[16] and are provided by 'non-mandated' agencies as a matter of course. Many of the families that take advantage of the services provided by 'non-mandated' agencies are Aboriginal[17] families, and I will attempt to provide some background and explanation for this below. It means, however, that while some families can work 'in partnership' with child welfare workers who do not have the authority to take their children away, many people must operate within the framework of a potentially coercive relationship in which the fear of their children's possible apprehension is always present. It is the provisions for voluntary services by, and agreements with 'mandated' agencies on which I intend to concentrate my reflections on partnership.

It seems therefore, that while the familiar themes of parental responsibility, welfare and partnership reveal themselves in the philosophy and specifics of the Manitoba CFS Act, they do so with nuances slightly different from those in the United Kingdom, but in ways which nevertheless may be instructive for English practitioners. As in the United Kingdom, however, the relationship in Manitoba between these principles is complicated (Bainham, 1990b) and the tension between them may create tensions for workers and families applying them.[18] In Manitoba the CFS Act has been in force since 1986, and in some provinces, provisions for voluntary services have been operative for ten years or more. All of the people working with such legislation have therefore been working 'in partnership' for all of that time. In some ways they have been extremely successful in meeting the goals of co-operation with, and empowerment of, families. In other ways, however, the lofty goals of partnership have been elusive or have been found simply to be impossible to achieve. Either way, while much of the law and practice cannot blithely be transplanted from Canada to the UK without losing most, if not all, of its relevance, there may be some insights of relevance to English child protection practitioners which can usefully be gained. This chapter is an attempt, therefore, to introduce some of those Canadian experiences to an English legal and social work audience, and will reflect upon some of the lessons we have learned in Canada. I do not wish to provide a 'table of concordance' for readers; rather I wish to identify three or four of those practices within the 'partnership principle' which have been successfully integrated into social work and legal discourse, and those that have been more problematic. As I have in the past occupied both spaces, my enquiry will proceed from both a practical and an academic perspective. Further, as I am most familiar with the law and practice in the province of Manitoba, that jurisdiction will be the main focus of my comments.

Specifically, I wish to confront the legal, political and philo-sophical ideology reflected in the pre-eminence given to 'voluntary support' or partnership principles in the legislation. I want tentatively to problematise the political and social implications of a policy which appears to be based upon the individualisation and privatisation of the family and then to explore what this means for partnership in an increasingly rights-conscious society. Secondly, and following from the first discussion, I hope to address some of the problems which can arise from attempting to reconcile principles of voluntary co-operation with those that construct care proceedings as adversarial, including the creation of the 'dual role' for child care workers. Finally, although there is no comparable reference to partnership principles in Manitoba legislation after a care order is made by the court in favour of a child care agency, there is a statutory requirement that questions of contact between parents and children in care be agreed between agencies and parents. I will examine the symbolic and the practical value of proclaiming even this type of diluted, or reformulated, partnership at this post-order stage.

The 'voluntary service' philosophy

The replacement, in 1986, of the Manitoba Child Welfare Act[19] by the Child and Family Services Act was part of a trend across most of the Canadian provinces to reshape not only the practice, but also the philosophy of child protection. The 'child saving' interventionist philosophies of the 1960s increasingly became seen in the 1980s as unwarranted intervention in the autonomy of families, a shift noticed by writers such as Thompson (1988:16) who wrote of the almost subtle change in discourse from 'child welfare' to 'child protection'. Similarly, Parton (1991) describes the shift in the United Kingdom as one from a medico-social focus on child abuse to a socio-legal focus on child protection, in which law helps to constitute both what the problem is and what should be done about it. In effect, the shift has reinforced the public/private dichotomy in both social and legal discourse but, paradoxically, at the same time as law's public/private divide in this way became more entrenched in the discourse of child protection in Manitoba, the statute itself took on the name of the Child and Family **Services** Act. It seemed that despite the shift in emphasis, welfare was still on the agenda, only now the family was not to be investigated and assistance provided coercively, support was to be provided for families voluntarily, and in co-operation with child care agencies.

On the one hand, this shift in philosophy appears to be consistent with a liberal social policy of respect for the autonomy of the family, and to be designed to promote the family's status as the fundamental private institution of society. 'Involuntary' state intervention in the family, in the form of agency intervention, was no longer justified on vague 'welfare' grounds: now it was only reasonable on strict 'protection' grounds. It needed to be justified according to clear legislative criteria, and the new statutes provided for legal representation for all parties (including the child) and the confirmation of many of the procedural requirements of what is known in North America as 'due process' (Bala, 1991: 4-6). The state was, in effect, washing its hands of responsibility for the welfare of families except in narrowly defined circumstances when children required protection or were 'in need'. It is important to realise, however, that this shift in discourse was more subtle in jurisdictions like Manitoba than it was in England and Wales with the proclamation of the Children Act 1989. For example, while the old

Child Welfare Act of 1974 spoke in terms of 'welfare', due process for parents in cases of coercive intervention was still provided for, whereas many of the provisions of the (now repealed) Children and Young Persons Act 1969 did not even recognise parents as parties to an adversarial process.

On the other hand, the emphasis in recent legislation in both the UK and Canada on voluntary, preventative services may, in fact, belie the privacy rhetoric on the surface of the legislation. In this volume, King and Kaganas have reinforced the argument that the state's supervisory power may be increased rather than decreased by its enhanced capacity to monitor, supervise and support families. Further, this supervisory power is potentially expanded when exercised in partnership, outside of the purview of court scrutiny and public accountability (Wildgoose, 1987).

Nevertheless, the ideological significance of maintaining the rhetoric of public and private and of valorising the private family is great. Margaret Thatcher's pronouncement that there is no such thing as society, there are only individuals and there are families, speaks to political concerns to privatise not only the (cost of) care for (and of) members of a family, but also to obscure the interdependence of the family/state relationship. It implies that, within the limits laid down by law, whatever happens within a family, including its 'successes' and its 'failures', is the private responsibility of that family. In a society which has internalised that philosophy, parents and social workers would have great difficulty perceiving themselves as equals, and services to families, even when provided voluntarily, will always be haunted by the spectre of failure and blame. Entrenchment of a dichotomy between public and private only reinforces beliefs that when the state does intervene, even co-operatively, in the realm of the 'private', something must be wrong, and that something can only be located within the dynamics, or the relationships, or the personalities of the family members. 'Irrespective of the nature and strengths of the pressure exerted by structural variables on the family, [this] analysis of family failure [remains] grounded at the level of individual behaviour' (Lewis, 1986, quoted in David, 1991b:111) and becomes accepted as reality by both families and the state alike. In this ideological context state assistance in the form of family centres, counselling, parent aides and home-makers becomes part of a privatised, consumerist self-help scheme (David, 1991b), offered to families to 'improve themselves' and to 'become less dependent' (see Cannan, 1992).

Furthermore, creating and entrenching a dichotomy between public and private in this way perpetuates the continued subordination of women, a perspective which is missing from much of the political debate concerning social policy (David, 1991b).

The elaboration in legal discourse of a private domain of subjectivity, morality and the personal as 'not the law's business' has inevitably led to non-intervention in domestic life....One implication is that those confined to the domestic sphere need not look to law to rectify any power imbalance....(O'Donovan, 1985:11).

Supporters of radical 'family autonomy' philosophy tend to overlook the fact that 'the nuclear family which they so admire reflects a particular culture within a particular set of social relations: it is the family form of the bourgeoisie' (O'Donovan, 1985:15), and includes within it restrictive and subordinating definitions of 'proper' gender roles (David, 1991b). Family autonomy is promoted by reference to 'natural' morality which often translates into traditional patriarchal morality. In this ideological context, the Manitoba Act, with its parent aide and skills training schemes, and the English Act, with the educatory role allowed to the various home visitors and to family centres, are both concerned to legalise this philosophy and the reproduction of particular kinds of families in which each member's role conforms to 'natural' or 'traditional' ones (Cannan, 1992; David, 1991b).

Along with privatisation of the family in contemporary legal and social discourse, is the valorisation of rights (Bala, 1991; Smith, 1991). In Canada the Charter of Rights is amenable to use in many legal contexts, and in the United Kingdom more and more reference is made to the European Convention on Human Rights. What is important here is not how these documents are made use of, but rather their ideological influence on families and the provision of services to families. In societies which define themselves as collections of individuals, each having autonomous rights to be protected, the relationship between the family and the state comes to be defined by negative rights whereby the autonomous family claims a right to be protected from an intrusive state, rather than by notions of interdependence, co-operation and mutuality in which the family has a right to be assisted by a responsible state.[20]

My point in problematising the politics of child care legislation in this way is to confront the ideological nature of child protection law and practice and to situate it in a particular social and legal context. Philosophies of privacy and of rights mediate any potential partnership relationship between the state and families.

Reconciling the principles in practice

1.

It is only within its social and ideological context that we can examine the 'hard law' (Yard, 1990) of the statutes. Autonomy, rights and due process ideology, along with much statute and case law, frame child protection matters as adversarial in nature. Concurrently, certain provisions of those same statutes and service/

partnership ideology allow social workers to provide a voluntary, but nonetheless intrusive helpful hand in family affairs. Indeed, the guiding principles behind such a dual philosophy would seem to require in the legislation a broad scope for voluntary services to be provided in partnership with parents, along with careful guidelines for any agreements made respecting those services, and restrictive criteria for apprehension of children in case those services fail (Barnhorst and Walter, 1991). These foundations do not appear in either the Children Act 1989 or the Manitoba CFS Act, however. In the Children Act, although there are somewhat restrictive criteria for the Act's equivalent of the 'apprehension' of children, local authorities have a duty to provide voluntary services only for families whom they define as 'in need'[21], and in fact many of the services which are preventative in nature (such as housing or health services) are often not part of the local authority's remit at all.

The expected legislative foundations of the dual philosophy of autonomy/due process and service/partnership are not clearly evident in Manitoba, either. Not only are the criteria for apprehension of children fairly broad, but guidelines for provision of voluntary services to families seem to be left within the broad discretion of social workers. Recent anecdotal evidence suggests that lack of funding, which has led to increasingly long waiting lists for services such as counselling and skills training schemes has affected the exercise of social worker discretion in that rather than undertake any risk, children may be apprehended while their parents wait for these 'voluntary' services to become available. Indeed, it is the initial exercise of social worker discretion which forms the nature of most agency/family relationships.

Lord Justice Butler-Sloss recognised the potential conflict for workers between the two philosophical pressures of autonomy/due process and service/partnership, and in the aftermath of the Cleveland crisis, was anxious that local authorities (re)define workers' roles in its light.

> Social Services whilst putting the needs of the child first must respect the rights of the parents; they also must work if possible with the parents for the benefit of the children. These parents themselves are often in need of help. Inevitably a degree of conflict develops between those objectives. (Butler-Sloss, 1988:244, para.16).

One writer suggests that this means that social workers must perform a 'dual' role and that this dual role contributes to the high incidence of stress and the high turnover rate among child protection workers in Canada (Bala, 1991). Certainly there is an inevitable tension between the worker's 'supportive' role of therapist, counsellor, educator and administrator for provision of other services, and his or her 'investigative' child protection role akin to that of police officer in a criminal investigation (Bala, 1991: 9). Is the role most accurately described as 'dual', however, or is it

fundamentally an irreconcilable conflict of interest which is anti-
thetical to achieving true partnership even at this early stage in the
agency/family relationship?

Practice under both the Manitoba Act with its mixed philo-
sophical thrust, and the Ontario Act, which is said to follow a purer
due process model (Bala, 1991), means that even if agency
involvement is initially voluntarily accepted, in the event of later
difficulties, anything a parent or child has done or said becomes
relevant and admissible in evidence to justify an apprehension or to
support an agency application for guardianship in a subsequent
protection hearing. Thus, child care workers are advised to record,
listen and observe in an objective manner (Vogl, 1991) at the same
time as they must advise, counsel and assist families. It is not
surprising that many families are inhibited by this 'dual' role from
most effectively making use of their case worker's support, in effect,
frustrating the whole idea of partnership. Case workers are often
regarded with distrust and suspicion by parents (Wildgoose, 1987),
and not only are distrust and suspicion barriers to a successful
partnership arrangement, they also are easily reinterpreted to mean
unco-operativeness. Kaganas in this volume, describes some of the
possible implications for families under the Children Act of being
labelled 'unco-operative', and experience in Manitoba suggests as
well, that if parents refuse or question any of the recommendations
of agency workers, they risk apprehension of their children. Lack of
co-operation with agencies at this stage often works against
families in subsequent court proceedings as well. In *Re C*[22], a 1979
Ontario decision, the judge criticised counsel who instructed his
client not to talk to agency workers for fear that her statements
would be used against her in court, implying that a parent's role in
the partnership is to co-operate with the agency by, among other
things, making full disclosure, and that counsel's role is to facilitate,
or at least not to inhibit, that disclosure.

Given these difficulties, the voluntary nature of the partnership
between parents and workers is often undermined as soon as the
worker is invited into the family home. Immediately the spectre of
investigation and potential apprehension appears (Thompson,
1989a), and both of the worker's hats become alarmingly visible to
parents. In order to provide appropriate assistance, workers must
enquire as to the difficulties the family is facing, and in order to
properly assess the degree of risk, they must keep records of the
information provided. As stated, the family is not in a position to
censor the information they provide for fear of being labelled 'unco-
operative' or for fear of inhibiting the benefits they can gain from
the agency. The investigatory powers of child care workers are,
unlike those of police officers, unregulated, and here there is no
semblance of a right to silence or of protection from self incrimina-
tion (Thompson, 1989a). Rather, self-incrimination is expected.

Additionally, not only are families and agencies working in

partnership with one another, the resources of a broad community base are often called upon to provide support for a family. Hospital workers, public health workers, school teachers, psychologists, police officers, counsellors, therapists and religious advisers all may become a part of the support plan for a family, and once again parents and children are placed in an invidious position. 'Failure to co-operate and "bare their souls" with these individuals' may tip the balance from voluntary to involuntary intervention, and if it gets to court, 'may well sink their case, as such co-operation and full disclosure is viewed as critical by most agency workers and judges' (Thompson, 1989a) as we saw in the *Re C* case. Further, parents must always be wary, as if they do 'bare their souls' to a number of these potential witnesses, it is almost certain that their comments will be preserved in note form. Parents ought to be aware that should the matter be taken to court, their comments can become interpreted as admissions, and usually:

> those to whom admissions are made are 'professional note takers', while the makers of the admissions rarely carry notebooks with them. The result? The contest becomes one of official black and white notes versus fuzzy parental memories. (Thompson, 1989a:242)

Thompson reminds us further of the unconscious mental editing of notes: the inevitable tendency to record the unusual, the worrying and the damaging, but not the ordinary, the positive, or the self serving (1989a:242).

It is ironic that agency support, which could be the most effective means of assisting families and preventing the removal of children from their homes, is inhibited by fear that voluntarily accepted intervention too quickly turns into involuntary intervention, and in consequence legal advice to parents is often not to approach mandated agencies for assistance at all. It was sometimes thought by parents and lawyers alike that the worst thing a troubled family could do was to make the agency aware of its existence. Their fear was not an unreasonable one, given research findings in Ontario which showed that in approximately 90 percent of protection cases which ended up in court, there was "previous agency involvement" with the family (Wildgoose, 1987).[23] These findings, coupled with the expectations of courts regarding parental co-operation with agencies suggests that an agency's unregulated supervisory power over family autonomy is great, and is potentially enhanced by use of principles of partnership and mutuality. Consideration, then, of the true voluntariness of service plans must always include acknowledgement of the ever-present spectre of apprehension which is enhanced by an agency's dual role with families.

The above empirical observations further demonstrate the gap between public deference to an ideology of family autonomy, and social work and legal practice (Wildgoose, 1987). Vogl (1991) notes the social worker's traditional professional preference for assuming the therapist/advice role over the investigatory one, and Wildgoose (1987) posits that agencies' broad child-centred approaches to family services lead an agency to tend to 'arrogate to itself the widest latitude and maximum control and autonomy in the method and duration of intervention into the family unit' (p.66). Her study found that even in a jurisdiction such as Ontario, with its legislative emphasis on autonomy/due process, there was a general lack of participation by parents in all stages of proceedings, from initial involvement to court disposition. It is easy to criticise social workers for an overly coercive or interventionist strategy despite policies encouraging parental autonomy, or to blame training which instils in them 'rescue fantasies' (Wildgoose, 1987:67) or paternalism, but it must be noted that courts collude to some degree in the disempowerment of parents when they require parents to 'co-operate' with social workers and fail to demand accountability for 'voluntary' agency actions.

2.

The Children Act 1989 does not provide specifically for written agreements between parents and local authorities, but such written agreements are contemplated as being part of good social work practice and are specifically referred to in the Arrangements for Placement of Children Regulations to the Children Act 1989. The concept of written agreements is consistent with partnership principles in which both parties to the partnership have a clear understanding of the goals and objectives of the partnership. Manitoba legislation confirms both this practice and the province's due process philosophy by providing that agreements for voluntary services, including voluntary placement outside the parents' home, may be made on forms prescribed by the regulations.[24] As two writers say, 'Ideally, legislation would contain provisions that ensure that the agreement is truly voluntary... and that the agreement is clear as to what services will be provided' (Barnhorst and Walter, 1991:23-24). On examination of the forms prescribed by the Manitoba regulations, however, we see that the agreements are cursory, brief, and surprisingly lacking in detail. For example, the form allowing for the placement of a home-maker or parent aide simply says:

Whereas the above applicants are requesting home-maker/
parent aide services to assist in caring for the child(ren) listed
below....

Now therefore the parties agree as follows:

1. In accordance with the *Child and Family Services Act* the
agency agrees to place a home-maker/parent aide in the home
of the applicant for not less than ..... hours per day, ... days
per week, the placement to begin on the ..... day of and
continue until the ..... day of ....., a period not exceeding 6
months.

2. The applicant(s) consent(s) to the placement of the home-
maker/parent aide to look after and care for the child(ren)
named herein and in consideration of the services to be
provided agree to pay to the agency the amount of ..... dollars
per month of service.

(From Form 6 – Family Support Service Agreement, Man Reg 57/86.
The balance of the form deals with provision for payment and
renewal and termination of the agreement.)

The form leaves open questions as to what the home-maker is
actually supposed to do in the home. This information is left to be
clarified outside of the document. Difficulties which can arise when
any agreement is not sufficiently clear or specific can arise then,
even where there is a required form of contract. These difficulties
can be illustrated by one case, in which a Manitoba woman
approached Child and Family Services of Central Winnipeg for help
with her two children. The agency arranged for a home-maker for
her, but this proved to be of no assistance, as

> the expectations which Ms H had for the home-maker were at odds with
> the purpose for which the Agency had put her there. It appears that not
> enough time was taken to fully explain to Ms H what role the home-
> maker could play.[25]

It seems that 'good social work practice' was not adhered to in this
case but it is also an example of the second reason proffered to
social workers for completing written agreements. They offer 'an
example of the dual helper/enforcer role. The preparation of such a
contract not only represents co-operative planning with a family, it
also anticipates later court involvement' (Vogl, 1991:42). If the goals
of the agreement are not met, the agreement itself may be an
important piece of evidence justifying court intervention. In this
case, the agency did not hesitate to call the court's attention to the
fact that the home-maker agreement failed. In many cases the

home-maker herself (and they are virtually always women) is called as an agency witness.

A second observation regarding the Manitoba forms, is that despite the importance of these documents, and despite the fact that they are rarely executed after review by or in the presence of counsel for the parents,[26] words such as 'whereas', 'herein', 'thereof' and 'in consideration of' seem to be used with no regard to the confusing and even intimidating effect such 'legalese' can have upon lay people, particularly people in the midst of a family crisis. Moreover, the agreements must be witnessed, but there is no provision for the witness' affidavit which could attest to the true voluntariness of the signatures. In contrast, the Ontario legislation attempts to ensure that all agreements are voluntary[27] and are entered into with full knowledge of their implications.[28]

Finally, it is significant and illustrative of family autonomy/ voluntary assistance ideology that the 'applicants' are said in the Manitoba agreement to be 'requesting' services from the agency, for which they then agree to pay. Once more, this language reinforces notions of private responsibility, consumerism and self-help, and obscures both any duty the state may have to assist, and the possibility of unintended or intended agency coercion when the home-maker arrangement is first discussed with the family.

Others have suggested that carefully detailed agreements may in fact work against parents even with the best intentions of social workers (see Kaganas in this volume). From the point of view of busy professionals like lawyers and social workers, arranging one's day or one's week around various appointments and meetings is an (unfortunate but) ordinary way to live. From the point of view of parents, (many of whom do not own Filofaxes or have easy access to transport) required attendance at appointments with numerous different professionals and service bureaucracies is difficult, intrusive and often resented as a manipulation of power on the part of the agency. More than one client complained to me that she felt she was being set up to fail by a well meaning agency social worker who simply could not believe that she did not have the bus fare to get to her many scheduled appointments.

Another difficulty with relying on written agreements too heavily is the nature of their formation and interpretation. It is understood that if contracts for voluntary services are entered into, the traditional prerequisites for the valid execution and enforcement of contracts generally are applicable (Wilson and Tomlinson, 1986). So, for example, an agreement may be set aside if it is entered into under duress, through coercion, or specifically under the threat of the agency's apprehension of the child (Wilson and Tomlinson, 1986). This, of course, begs the question as to the applicability of traditional contract doctrine in the child protection context. One feminist analysis of contract doctrine, for example, suggests that the law does not recognise a contracting individual's contextual reality, but rather assumes contracting parties to be free, unencumbered, self-interested, assertive and autonomous, and that this assumption, far from being objective and neutral, privileges the reality of men over that of women, particularly women with children.[29] This analysis would mean that traditional concepts such as duress may be particularly inapplicable to child welfare agreements, and yet these agreements are routinely used in Canada, are advocated in England, and are assumed by law to be voluntarily and freely entered into.

3.

Along with the right to obtain voluntary services from child care agencies should come the right to refuse such services, but as I discussed earlier, refusal of services can be interpreted as uncooperativeness. Agencies in Canada are aware, however, of issues of family autonomy and of the requirements of due process in their governing statutes.

> Given the authority of the child protection agency to remove children if necessary, it is not surprising that families often do not realize their right to decline services of the child protection agency. It is only with legal advice that a family can accurately determine the legal authority of the intervening agency. **It is important for a protection worker to respect and even encourage use of a family's right to seek legal advice at any stage of involvement.** (emphasis added) (Vogl, 1991:42)

It is here as well that the state's apparent commitment to its due process/autonomy philosophy can be tested. While practising law in Manitoba, in addition to the Legal Aid Certificates I received authorising me to represent parents who wished, in the words of the authorisation, to 'oppose CFS application for guardianship', I also received a number of 'advise and assist' certificates. Such authorisations from Legal Aid Manitoba are similar to the Green Form scheme in the United Kingdom. 'Advise and assist' certificates were issued by Legal Aid Manitoba at the request of parents before any formal apprehension of their children, usually at the stage of an agency wishing to negotiate with them an agreement for voluntary temporary placement of their children, or when other arrangements regarding accommodation were being discussed. It is significant that Legal Aid Manitoba typically does not issue 'advise and assist' certificates when home-maker, parent aide or day care agreements are contemplated, although its policy does not preclude this. Instead, those few parents requesting advice and information regarding home-maker or parent aide agreements are generally referred to Legal Aid's 'drop in' programme, in which advice is given on an informal basis. Counsel normally becomes formally involved only after the parent aide or home-maker agreement has failed and it becomes necessary to discuss the child's removal from home. Perhaps this pattern has developed because parents are reluctant to stand on their right to counsel at this early stage, fearing that requesting Legal Aid assistance may in some way undermine their appearance of good faith. Perhaps parents are not aware of their right, or interest, in having an advocate during this agreement stage, or perhaps contact with Legal Aid is discouraged by agency workers. It is submitted that co-operation and partnership can be more of a reality only when some of the imbalance of power is redressed by the presence of an advocate (who need not be a lawyer, and sometimes that role is undertaken by a worker from a 'non-mandated' agency) for the parents at all stages of agency involvement, and that agencies must accept that the presence of an advocate does not cast doubt on a family's good faith or desire to work in partnership.

June Thoburn (1991a) has suggested that partnership under the Children Act is not an idealistic and unattainable goal, and she identifies a shift in social work training and philosophy to be necessary to achieve what the Act sets out. Evidence from 7 – 10 years of experience in Canada however, seems to indicate that neither the courts nor agencies have yet taken all steps toward furthering the balance of family autonomy and partnership which prevailing child welfare discourse would require of them. The legislation leaves a vast range of discretion to child care professionals, and is approved by the courts at the same time as family autonomy is 'recognized' in the legislation.[30] As Michael King suggests in this book, privacy and rights are only conditional in the child protection context, they can be overridden by social workers, and, I would add, by courts. Moreover, the privatisation philosophy discussed earlier leads to perceptions that parents in the system are there because of some deficiency or fault on their part, and work with these families is further complicated by the statistics which show that those parents in the system often come from the least articulate and least educated segments of society. In this light, an unrepresented parent simply does not have the leverage to approach even one of Thoburn's new and differently trained agency workers as a partner. Communication between them would often, as before, be thwarted by language, class and cultural differences (Wildgoose, 1987).

It is submitted that nowhere is this more strikingly illustrated than by the experience of First Nations families in Manitoba. From the 1950s to the 1980s, Aboriginal children were apprehended in alarmingly disproportionate numbers to children of families of European origin, to the extent that one judge referred to the phenomenon as 'cultural genocide' (Kimmelman, 1985). First Nations homes and child rearing practices were too often seen during this period by an interventionist social work community as being 'unfit' when compared with Western, European nuclear family standards. An inquiry established in 1990 to examine the justice system and Aboriginal peoples put the solution in these terms:

The non-mandated Ma Mawi Chi Itata Centre was established in 1984 to serve Aboriginal families in Winnipeg as a result of the determined effort by Aboriginal people to remove services for Aboriginal families and children from the Children's Aid Society of Winnipeg. Aboriginal people were convinced that the CAS was more interested in apprehending children than in providing support to parents to help keep their families together....Ma Mawi did not replace the mandated services of other non-Aboriginal agencies in the city, but rather extended and complemented them. Most Aboriginal people tend to trust Ma Mawi more than the other agencies, perhaps because Ma Mawi is not mandated and, therefore, cannot apprehend their children.... Aboriginal agencies are more sensitive to Aboriginal culture and the needs of families. They are sometimes able to find solutions which those not familiar with the community might not even consider (Report of the Aboriginal Justice Inquiry (AJI), 1991:529).

Thus, the solution to what was partly a communication crisis in Manitoba was to establish 'mandated' and 'non-mandated' Aboriginal agencies staffed by workers who were sensitive to and familiar with the Aboriginal view of 'best interests of the child'. This view 'takes into account the needs of the family and the community' (AJI, 1991:529) and does not privilege or normalise the status of the private, nuclear family. Nor does it ignore structural and social variables in contributing to the 'health' of the family. The Aboriginal view is that: 'in many cases the extended family encompasses the whole community. For Aboriginal agencies, the health of the community is an important factor in addressing the best interests of the child' (AJI, 1991:530).

While the establishment of Aboriginal agencies in Manitoba has gone some way to promote partnership principles between service agencies and Aboriginal families, it was a specific measure designed to deal with a specific, tragic reality.[31] Workers in non-Aboriginal mandated agencies still find themselves faced with barriers to communication and mutual understanding which only the most sensitive and extensive training can even begin to overcome.

Post-order partnership?

In Manitoba, principles of partnership do not extend beyond the making of a court order as they do under the Children Act 1989. There, a court order has the effect of transferring guardianship to the agency for the duration of the order. In contrast, the Children Act provides that parents maintain their parental responsibility after a care order is made. In Manitoba, then, while family autonomy is pursued in a partnership forged in the pre-apprehension relationship, there is no further attempt to create such a post-apprehension or post-order partnership. At this later

stage, service/partnership rhetoric is abandoned. Given the difficulties created by the inequality of power between the potential
partners at the voluntary service stage, it is submitted that the
Manitoba approach is a more honest and realistic one than the
English approach which seeks to portray post-order care as a
mutual undertaking.

This approach may be evidence of the United Kingdom's
stronger ideological commitment to private parental responsibility,
but once again, practice in both jurisdictions must be explored to
assess its relationship with stated principles. It is submitted that
while it does not maintain the language of parental responsibility at
this stage, the Manitoba Act in fact promotes the other side of the
autonomy/due process coin. It makes it clear that the agency is in
charge at the post-apprehension and post-order stage, but then
states that parental access to children in care must be reasonable,
and further that where parents and agency fail to agree on what is
reasonable, the onus is on the agency to demonstrate the reason-
ableness of its proposed limitation of access.[32] In contrast, the
Children Act 1989, after proclaiming that parents retain parental
responsibility after a court order is pronounced, goes on to say that
a local authority has the power 'to determine the extent to which a
parent or guardian of the child may meet his parental responsibility
for him'[33] and, although there is a presumption in favour of
reasonable contact, there is no statutory right to challenge the local
authority's other decisions.[34] The Manitoba legislation subordin-
ates 'privacy' philosophy to 'due process' philosophy at this stage,
and it is in this context that a different notion of partnership is
constructed. It is a notion of 'involuntary' rather than 'voluntary'
partnership, but unlike the involuntary partnership required by the
Children Act 1989, it is given teeth by the equally strong Canadian
commitment to rights and due process. Experience in Manitoba
suggests that courts take seriously the burden placed upon agencies
at this stage to initiate access discussions with parents[35] and that
because of the requirement to agree to terms of contact, agencies
must justify to parents and their counsel any limitations they seek
to place on access. It is significant that the parties' bargaining
power is usually more balanced by the time these negotiations take
place, as by this time parents' counsel is usually involved. This
approach can be contrasted with that of the Children Act 1989, in
which a symbolic notion of parental responsibility is offered as a
substitute for any practical, rights-based applications of it, which, I
submit, makes non-voluntary partnership under the 1989 Act more
difficult to achieve, if not merely an ideologically motivated
chimera.

Conclusions

The ideological context of both jurisdictions is one of privacy/
autonomy/due process for the family, at the same time as the

welfare/best interests of children are said to be paramount. This creates a conflict for child welfare practitioners, and evidence from Canada shows that social work practice is often difficult to reconcile with the stated ideological commitment. The result in pre-apprehension situations is often that, by employing principles of service/partnership, interventionism is exercised in fact, privacy in principle. Partnership in this context appears to keep family privacy intact, but in reality gives more supervisory power to the state. It breaks down the public/private barrier in practice (King, in this volume), at the same time as public policy entrenches and celebrates that divide. Ironically, in Manitoba, it is when pure privacy principles are subordinated, that due process allows a form of (albeit non-voluntary) partnership to work most clearly.

It is unfortunate that factors within the system seem to be conspiring against true agency/parent partnership in the care of children in Manitoba. Despite their best intentions, there always seems to be a 'one up/one down' relationship between social workers and parents which militates against the provision of a truly voluntary service. This is not to say that voluntary partnership can never work; the vast number of cases that are not reported and do not end up contested in court means that voluntary services may be effective in assisting many families, but it would take a survey of parental feelings to assess the degree of coercion they felt in accepting those services, and the degree of blame they felt for their situation of need to evaluate the broader social implications of the principle.

Lessons from Canada for the short term may suggest that making better use of the equivalent of non-mandated agencies (such as Family Centres – see Cannan, 1992:Ch 6) in support and service plans, structuring vastly refocused training for social workers, and providing for advocates for parents and for accountability of workers at all stages of proceedings may help to promote a more 'honest' partnership. By making this statement I am not suggesting that an 'honest' partnership requires complete equality between the parties, but I am suggesting, as does Kaganas in this book, that it is a complicated relationship which requires some mutuality of goals, openness of communication, and at least a minimal degree of trust. As Thompson suggests, (1989a) some type of warning for families that the things they tell their support workers may later be repeated against them may help to diffuse the sense of unfairness or betrayal they feel on hearing it repeated in court, but this may only serve to undermine the working relationship between worker and parent. It is at this point that we must ask ourselves the unstated but implicit question which underpins this chapter: whether this working partnership relationship is one we want to pretend to maintain in its current ideological context. Does the political rhetoric of family autonomy together with an unproblematised, somewhat romantic view of partnership have any value other than to make more palatable government policy designed to deepen the public/private divide and to construct a particular family form as both 'real' and desirable?

Postscript

Legal Aid Manitoba has recently announced plans to restructure its services to child welfare clients. Henceforth, when apprehended children are the subject of court proceedings, documents served on respondents will encourage them to contact a newly established Legal Aid Child Welfare Office for assistance, and particulars of all agency apprehensions and terms of orders being sought will be directed from the apprehending agency to that office.

Notes

1. Schedule B to the Constitution Act 1982.
2. R.S.O. 1990 c. C11.
3. S.M. 1985-86, c.8. (C.C.S.M.C80).
4. See, for example, the Declaration of Principles at the beginning of the legislation.
5. It then goes on to provide a list of circumstances in which children are deemed to be in need of protection.
6. Section 32 states that while a demand can be made of the agency for particulars of the grounds which are alleged to justify a finding that a child is in need of protection, the rules of the Court of Queen's Bench regarding examination for discovery and examination of documents do not apply to a child protection hearing.
7. Section 35.
8. Apprehension of a child usually involves his or her removal from the home, but the Act also provides for 'deemed apprehensions' whereby the worker or officer may leave the child with or return the child to the person in whose charge the child was, and that child shall be deemed to be under apprehension (s26 Child and Family Services Act).
9. Section 2 (1) of the Manitoba Act states that 'the best interest of the child shall be the paramount consideration of the director, an agency and a court in all proceedings under this Act affecting a child, other than proceedings to determine whether a child is in need of protection...'. It then goes on to provide a list of factors to be considered in determining best interests.
10. See for example, Alberta, Child Welfare Act 1984; British Columbia, Family and Child Service Act 1980; and Newfoundland, Child Welfare Act 1972.
11. See, for example, Manitoba, The Child and Family Services Act 1985-86; Ontario, The Child and Family Services Act 1984; Prince Edward Island, Family and Child Services Act 1988; Saskatchewan, The Child and Family Services Act 1989-90.
12. Child and Family Services Act, (hereafter called CFS Act) above, at note 3, s25.
13. Section 48 CFS Act.
14. Section 13(3) CFS Act.
15. Section 13(4) CFS Act.
16. Section 7(b) provides that agencies shall 'provide family counselling, guidance and other services to families for the prevention of circumstances requiring the placement of children in protective care or in treatment plans'.
17. By use of the term 'Aboriginal', I am referring to the people of Canada's First Nations, those who have historically been labelled by the non-Aboriginal majority as 'Indian' or 'Metis'.

18. See on the tensions between principles of welfare, protection and rights, Smith (1991).
19. SM 1974 c 30.
20. See Cannan, (1992) in the context of the educatory roles of family centres in Britain, and a comparative analysis of the family – state relationship in Britain and France.
21. Section 17 Children Act 1989 (hereafter called CA 1989).
22. 2 FLR 18 (Ont. Prov. Ct.).
23. See Piper, Ch 3 in this volume for UK research showing that mothers' requests for help often led only to their 'surveillance' (at p.47).
24. Section 13(5) CFS Act.
25. *CFS* v. *K.H. and N.P.* (1991) Man. R. (2d) 155, at 157, per Mullally J.
26. See infra, Part 3.
    27.   Section 4, Child and Family Services Act, above at note 2.
28. *Ibid* s29(8).
29. See, for example, Frug (1992), Chapters 4, 5 and 6.
30. See, for example, *Central Winnipeg CFS* v. *SW and MW* (1987) 52 Man R (2d) 184; 11 RFL (3d) 289, per Helper J A at p. 290 where the court states that the Declaration of Principles at the beginning of the CFS Act, some of which declare the principle of the autonomy of families, 'amplifies the responsibilities' of the court. See also *CFS Winnipeg* v. *ACF et al.* (1993) 81 Man R (2d) 149, Helper JA at p.149, where she states that:
    > there is precious little evidence to support a finding that the best interests of this child will be served by placing her permanently with her aunt K.F. I say that despite my support for the principles set forth in the Child and Family Services Act reciting the importance of maintaining a family unit and raising a child within his or her own family setting.
31. See further on First Nations child welfare, Kline (1992); Monture (1989) and Sinclair, Phillips and Bala (1991).
32. See Section 39(2) CFS Act concerning access during a temporary order of guardianship. The rules regarding access after apprehension but before an order are similar: ss27(2), (3) and (4).
33. Section 33 CA 1989.
34. The Act does provide, however, for an internal administrative complaints procedure for those who feel aggrieved by a local authority's decision. See S34 concerning contact.
35. See *Winnipeg Child and Family Services* v. *ACF and CEM and KF (Intervenor)* (1993) 80 Man R. (2d) 93, where the agency was admonished by the court for not initiating or facilitating access of a child to her aunt, the intervenor guardianship applicant.
    > The Agency suggested that the onus of obtaining visiting privileges should have been upon the aunt... I disagree. Section 27(2) of the Act places the onus on an Agency, after apprehending a child, to propose the access appropriate to the situation (p. 95).

    and further, at p. 97:
    > It must be accepted by a Child and Family Services Agency that it has an obligation to continue parental or family associations until the court has determined who will have responsibility to care for and raise the child.

    On appeal, (1993) 81 Man R. (2d) 149, the court clarified that after apprehension the statute required the agency to initiate and agree access to children not with all extended family members, but with parents or guardians.
    > I might add that under Section 27(2) of the Act the Agency is required to propose terms of access only to the parents of guardians of a child under apprehension. K.F. was neither the parent nor the guardian of the child at the time of apprehension. (per Helper J A).

Part C: Partnership in practice

5 Social work and families: lessons from research

June Thoburn

Introduction: defining partnership

The term 'partnership' itself does not appear in the Children Act 1989 but the requirement is clearly there to consult, and to give due consideration to the wishes and feelings of all family members and others who are important to the child. Consulting and giving due consideration certainly implies taking a step in the direction of partnership. In several places in the Guidance on the Act the word 'partnership' is mentioned but is not specifically defined.

> Partnership with parents and consultation with children on the basis of careful joint planning and agreement is the guiding principle for the provision of services within the family home and where children are provided with accommodation under voluntary arrangements (DoH, 1991e:para.2.1).

Working Together (DoH, 1991i:para.6.11) emphasises that this Guidance applies to child protection cases, and stresses:

> the importance of professionals working in partnership with parents and other family members or carers and the concept of parental responsibility. These principles must underpin all child protection work.

In a paper which forms part of a training pack commissioned by the Department of Health the following definition is used:

> It is marked by respect for one another, role divisions, rights to information, accountability, competence and value accorded to individual input. In short, each partner is seen as having something to contribute, power is shared, decisions are made jointly and roles are not only respected but also backed by legal and moral rights. (Tunnard, 1991:1)

This quote introduces the issue of power. Although this definition does not imply equality of power, it must be seriously questioned whether partnership is possible when power is so *unequally* divided, as it often is in the early stages of child protection work and when a child is in the care of the local authority by virtue of a care order.

This exploration of partnership in child protection work is based on two research studies, both funded by the Department of Health and both linked to wider programmes of research. It also draws on my experience as a consultant to guardians ad litem and as an expert witness in several contested cases following the implement-ation of the Act. These cases have given me the opportunity of considering the impact of the Act on planning for children in care, and especially on the questions of the return home of abused or neglected children; contact after long-term placement; and the respective merits of adoption or residence orders. In all these areas the principle of partnership is put to the test.

Two research studies

The first study, 'The Partnership in Child Protection study', examined the extent of family involvement in child protection work (Thoburn et al., 1995). The fieldwork straddled the implementation of the Children Act in 1991. The second, started in the autumn of 1992 and due for completion in mid-1995, is a study of the management and short-term (12 months) outcome of a cohort of child protection cases from areas in two counties and two London boroughs. The objectives of this study are to consider how the Children Act is working for children who are suffering, or are considered likely to suffer significant harm, as well as their families. A detailed study of about 50 children will be set in the context of all the cases which met the 'significant harm' criterion within the project areas during the data collection period. We are particularly interested to know:

- Whether the principles in the Act are being followed.

- Who are the decision makers.

- What the parents, children and professionals think about the process.

- What the outcome is for the child 12 months after the decision was taken that he or she is suffering or likely to suffer significant harm.

Cases are included in our sample mainly following child protection conferences, but we are also including any section 37 directions cases, and any child assessment orders or interim care applications which do not go through the conference system.

We do not anticipate that there will be many of these, but one example might be a case where an application is made for a care order in respect of a child who is already accommodated for reasons other than child protection.

This study has also given us information on services to children 'in need' because, firstly, a child 'in need of protection' is almost always a child 'in need' according to the Part III definition; and, secondly, in order to decide whether a case meets our criteria for inclusion in the sample, we are considering cases at the margins; both where a family receives services outside this significant harm threshold under the requirements of section 17, and where the case is closed after an investigation and no services are provided because it is considered that the 'significant harm' test does not apply.

The partnership in child protection study

Using Tunnard's definition we considered the extent to which family members were involved in the first six months of work following a child protection conference in 220 consecutive cases in seven English authorities. We chose these authorities because they all stated that they were attempting to work in partnership, although they did this in different ways. In 77 of the cases we had information from parents about the extent to which they considered that they had been involved. In 20 per cent of these at least one parent attended the whole of the child protection conference and in a further 17 per cent of cases at least one parent attended most of the initial child protection conference. As well as considering the involvement of the main parent, we were interested to know whether the children or young people themselves, and any non-resident parents, including alleged abusers, were involved in the process.

The first point to note is that, in common with many similar studies and national statistics (for example, Farmer and Owen, forthcoming; Gibbons et al., forthcoming; DoH, 1994) we found that the child's major residence for the six months following the conference was with a parent or parents in about three quarters of the cases. This included the alleged abuser in almost a half of the cases. In only one case in five was the child away from home for most of this period. Over half of the children lived with a mother only, with 36 per cent living with the mother and father or another partner, and 6 per cent with the father only. In 45 per cent of cases a female carer was alleged to have been involved in the maltreatment of the child, and in 55 per cent a male carer was alleged to have been involved. (In some cases male and female carers were involved jointly, and in a small minority of cases no carer was alleged to be involved). In looking at these figures one must allow for the fact that children were more at risk of abuse from mothers since more lived in households where a single mother was the carer.

Eighty-one per cent of the children were white, 10 per cent were of African, Caribbean or Asian descent, and 8 per cent were black children of mixed parentage. This last group appears to be over-represented, although it was not possible to ascertain the exact proportion of children from minority ethnic groups in the areas from which the sample was drawn.

In 61 per cent of the cases a decision was taken to register the index child (the oldest child in the family considered to be at risk). In 22 per cent of the 137 cases where a child was registered, the registration category was sexual abuse; in 44 per cent of cases it was physical abuse; the now defunct category of 'grave concern' was used in 19 per cent of cases; 6 per cent were registered in the emotional abuse group; and 9 per cent were registered in the neglect category.

This brief picture of 220 consecutive cases accords with the national picture and that emerging from other studies of child protection, except that a higher proportion of family members attended the conferences than was usually the case at that time.

The extent of family involvement in child protection

In assessing the extent to which family members were involved, we used a framework which took account of the degree of difficulty of the case. It was immediately apparent when we started our work that it would be easier for family members to be engaged in some cases than in others. Each case was therefore allocated to a 'best', 'middle' or 'worst' scenario group, for the purposes of working in partnership, according to a protocol drawn up by the research team in the light of earlier discussions. Cases were allocated to the 'best scenario' group if there was agreement between worker and parent about the extent of and culpability for the maltreatment; the alleged abuser was no longer living in the family home; the parent(s) were requesting help; and there was no history of violent behaviour or threats towards social workers. The 'worst scenario' group included cases where there was a history of violence or threats towards social workers and/or parents were not requesting help or there was no agreement about the extent of maltreatment or culpability for it. Those in the 'middle scenario' group had some features of the other two. It also became apparent that there were degrees of success in working in partnership, and that, in these early stages of child protection work, we would be unlikely to see many cases when, according to the Family Rights' Group definition, it would be possible for the work to be undertaken in partnership with family members.

Two research studies: summary of conclusions

In summarising the conclusions from both studies the different stages of intervention will be considered.

The threshold to a service

The section 17 threshold of 'in need' which entitles a child and his or her family to a service has been studied in more detail by Aldgate and Tunstill whose report is included in the Second Report on the Children Act (DoH, 1993a). Their report does not make encouraging reading. Voluntary groups (including self-help groups such as parents of children with disabilities) do not appear to have been widely consulted about the sorts of services which ought to be provided for children in need and their families.

Our two studies offer story after story of far from participatory practice at this threshold stage. If anything, the situation appears to be worse following the implementation of the Act than it was before. A common pattern is that families and young people who ask for help, especially those who are vulnerable by reason of homelessness, are turned away, only to be pulled into the system when things deteriorate and protection becomes a serious concern. In some cases it is the other professionals such as health visitors or teachers, and in other cases family members themselves, who feel obliged to exaggerate the risk of abuse in order to receive a service to which they have failed to gain access in other ways. The emphasis, in other words, has been placed on risk of harm at the hands of parents or carers, rather than on the extent of need and possible harm resulting from other sources.

To give one example, a young mother came to social services in a distressed state asking to see a social worker whom she had previously found very helpful. She said that she was becoming depressed again and would like to talk to the social worker who had previously helped her about the possibility of day care for her child. She was told that she could not see the same social worker as the case was closed, but should make an appointment to see the duty officer. On the same day her mother rang the department to say that she thought the child was being neglected owing to the mother's depressed state. At that point the case was allocated but not to the worker in whom the mother had confidence, but to a new worker who investigated the allegation of neglect through the child protection procedure.

The case of Mary and her 15 year old son Jamie, who helped us to pilot our research instruments for the present study, illustrates a similar point. Jamie, when he was seven, and his brother, were abused by Mary's cohabitee. After a very distressing period in care when he was again abused, this time by the son of the foster family, he returned to his mother at the age of ten. Not surprisingly, and despite early excellent support services on his return home, including attending a group for young people who had been abused, Jamie continued to have problems. By this time the case was closed, and his mother's attempts to get for him the supportive services which she and he had previously found helpful proved unsuccessful. Finally, in a 'planning meeting' which he found too painful, he ran out of the room and only then was he offered the accommodation which his mother had been requesting for several weeks. This story is little different from those reported by Fisher and colleagues in the In and Out of Care study which was influential in the implementation of the Act (Fisher et al., 1986). When Jamie completed the psychometric tests to help us with our current study, it became clear that he was seriously considering suicide and showed symptoms of depression.

Across the threshold of need

Once across the threshold of need, there are signs that there is more consultation, but still a tendency to use panels as a rationing device rather than as an opportunity to enter into full discussion with family members about the best way of helping and supporting them. This applies particularly to planning panels which are convened to discuss requests by parents and young people for accommodation for a child, or for day care or holidays. The notion of accommodation as a support service rather than as something to be avoided, which was so central to the philosophy of the Act, seems not yet to have been incorporated into everyday practice in most authorities. Jean Packman (whose study of children considered for care in two local authorities (Packman et al., 1986), had a major impact on the Act's emphasis on accommodation as a support service) is repeating that study in the same authorities so we shall learn more of whether there is substance in this impression.

There is a particularly difficult category of cases which fall into the uneasy area between section 17(b), those where a child is considered to be 'in need' because his or her health or development is likely to be significantly impaired without the provision of services under Part III of the Act, and those where a child is subject to investigation under section 47 because there is reason to believe that he or she is suffering significant harm or likely to suffer significant harm and the harm is due to the care given to him or her not being what it would be reasonable for a parent to give a similar child. In these cases there is considerable scope for interpretation and for a greater or lesser degree of parental involvement in determining the services needed. It is clear from our present study that in some authorities a service will be offered under section 17(b) while in others the case would be investigated under section 47. Figure 1, showing data from our second study, helps to clarify the position.

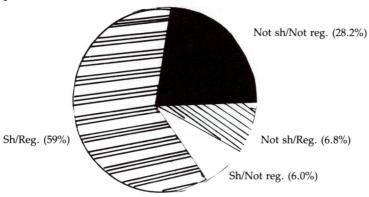

Not sh/Not reg. (28.2%)

Sh/Reg. (59%)

Not sh/Reg. (6.8%)

Sh/Not reg. (6.0%)

Sh – Significant harm
Reg. – Registered

Not sh – Not significant harm
Not reg. – Not registered.

Figure 1 Second Study: status of case following 117 initial child protection conferences in 4 local authorities

It gives details of 117 consecutive initial or incident child protection conferences held in areas of two county authorities and two London boroughs in 1993-1994. In seven per cent of the cases (one in 10 of those registered) it was decided to register a child when, in the view of the researchers, the significant harm or likely significant harm threshold was not crossed and it would have been more appropriate to help the child and family under section 17 provisions. There were seven cases (six per cent of those conferenced) where the child was, in the view of the researchers, suffering or likely to suffer significant harm but where the agency chose to provide services under section 17(b) and not use the child protection register system. It is part of our study to consider whether these differences can be attributed to factors in the cases themselves, perhaps relating to the willingness or otherwise of the family members to work with the local authority, or whether the differences were the result of different social work practice or agency policies. However, it does appear that although the route to services may be different, the services themselves are similar irrespective of the legislative label, and demonstrate a high degree of creativity in the use of resources and social work time made available under the provisions of Part III and Schedule 2 of the Act.

Partnership in child protection

Most studies of partnership in child protection work focus on the initial conference stage of the work, and the debate about partial or full attendance of parents continues and is resolved differently in different agencies. The impact of the attendance of the main carer or parent at child protection conferences has now been well researched, although most of the early studies involved only partial attendance.[2]

All such studies conclude that the balance of evidence is in favour of parental attendance at all or most of the conference. Parents generally comment that although they find attendance painful, they would much prefer to be there than to remain at home wondering what is happening. Professionals also usually comment favourably, although some still prefer to have family members excluded from certain parts of the conference. There are few studies of the systematic involvement of children and young people in conferences.

Our own study considered partnership more generally and looked at the involvement of parents, including non-resident parents, and children in other aspects of the procedures and in the social work practice. All the agencies studied stated that they were attempting to work in partnership. Table 1 gives the results in terms of the extent to which the practice of the worker and the policies of the agency were likely to lead to working in partnership with the main carer, the child, relatives, and non-resident parent.

Table 1   **The partnership in child protection study: researcher rating of agency procedures and social work practice in 220 consecutive child protection cases**

Practice/ policies likely to lead to working in partnership	With total sample		With main carer/parent		With child over ten		With relative		With non-resident parent	
	(n = 381)		(n = 217)		(n = 72)		(n = 13)		(n = 76)	
	No.	%	No.	%	No.	%	No.	%	No.	%
High/medium agency and social worker	193	51	115	53	37	51	9	69	30	39
High or medium agency/low social worker	23	6	16	7	4	6	2	15	1	1
High or medium social worker/low agency	104	27	57	26	18	25	2	15	26	34
Low agency and social worker	61	16	29	13	13	18	0	0	19	25

Based on protocols agreed by the researchers for the purposes of allocation to different categories with different degrees of participatory practice and procedures. From Thoburn et al. (1995)

Information was available from social workers, the records, and 102 members of 74 families about the extent to which, at one end of the continuum, they either participated or were partners, or, at the other extreme, they were not at all involved or were manipulated or placated. One of our major conclusions was that successful involvement of family members was associated both with procedures and with practice which were participatory. It was possible for workers who were highly motivated to involve family members, despite procedures which were less than helpful, as can be seen by the fact that in 34 per cent of cases where the agency had no policy for engaging non-resident parents, social workers nevertheless sought by their practice to involve them. Despite these best intentions, and in some cases carefully worked out procedures, it only proved possible to work in partnership with 3 per cent of the 378 family members involved in these cases, and in only 16 per cent of cases did we actually consider that there was significant participation. The proportion was higher if only the main carers and the children were considered.

Table 2   Summary of involvement of different family members in main decisions

Decision	Main parent(s)/carer(s)				Child over ten				Non-resident parent(s)				Significant relatives			
	PP		NI*		PP		NI*		PP		NI*		PP		NI*	
	N.	%	N.	%	N.	%	N.	%	N.	%	N.	%	N.	%	N.	%
About how investigation should be carried out	25	11	14	7	15	21	4	6	1	1	30	40	3	25	3	25
About risk of abuse or neglect	16	8	17	8	3	4	17	24	1	1	31	40	2	17	2	17
About registration	5	2	23	11	0	0	17	26	0	0	27	36	0	0	1	8
About care or accommodation	2	3	6	8	7	27	2	8	0	0	10	35	2	25	1	12
About protection plan	42	21	6	3	14	20	6	8	4	6	19	27	3	23	0	0
About help or services offered	39	21	9	5	15	24	8	13	4	6	22	35	4	33	1	8

NOTE: PP = Participated/were partners
NI* = Not involved – (includes categories 'involvement totally lacking', 'manipulation', 'placation').

Table 2 shows that children were most likely to be involved in decisions about how the investigation should be conducted. It was rare for any family member to be involved in the decisions about risk and registration; the main parents were more likely to be involved in decisions about the protection plan (21 per cent participated or were partners) and the help offered (again 21 per cent participated or·were partners). Children over ten were more likely than parents to participate in decisions about whether care or accommodation was appropriate and about the services to be offered. The findings from this research have many echoes in the smaller scale studies reviewed by Lewis (1992).

A framework devised by Howe (Figure 2) is helpful in under-standing why intention and effort is often not translated into the achievement of family member involvement.

Figure 2   A framework for the client/worker relationship

Status of client

		Involuntary	*Voluntary*
Participation	Absent	Strategic	Paternalism
	Present	Play Fair	Partnership

From Howe (1992:40).

He uses the dimensions of whether the agency and worker intend to work in partnership, and whether the family member is a voluntary or involuntary participant in the process. The following quotes from parents or social workers interviewed for our study illustrate these different groups of clients. In the strategic group are those who would prefer not to be clients and workers who made no attempt to involve the parent. As Howe puts it:

> The two players become strategists. They manoeuvre relative to the perceived position and intentions of the other. However, although trust and co-operation are often absent, particularly on the side of the unwilling client, the two parties understand the character of the relationship. (Howe, 1992:39)

> **Parent:** There is no partnership. It's them and us and they've got the power.

> **Peter aged 12:** All they do is ask you question after question after question. They did ask me if I wanted to answer the question. I didn't say 'no', because they would think I was rude. I just hoped it would finish soon.

The 'play fair' category includes cases where the parent does not request help but the worker tries to be open and honest about the process, and the parent co-operates in order to make the process as painless as possible.

> **Social Worker:** I share my findings and my opinions and intended actions with parents and attempt to negotiate an agreement on these and identify where we disagree.
> **Father:** Whether you agree or not, it is important that you are there to say what you want.

A paternalistic service is one in which, as Howe puts it, a 'parent requests help but is not encouraged to participate in the decision-making and helping process. The social worker remains the expert'. (1992:40)

> **Mother who attended only part of a conference:** The people involved just talked over me and said they would decide and let me know – which they didn't.
> **Father:** The social worker was only concerned about her own benefits and in doing her job correctly. No-one really cares about the parents in these situations.

For partnership along the lines of the Family Rights Group definition cited earlier to occur, according to Howe, the parent either needs to seek a service or accept that the service is necessary, and the social worker and agency must actively seek to involve the parent in the decisions and help. As Howe puts it: 'Although worker and client possess different knowledge and skills, they are active and equal partners in the relationship'. (1992:40)

> **Father:** That's what I like. I feel part of it. I don't feel pushed out of the way. Normally if I'm in a crowd I clam up if I don't know people.

Although we found this analysis helpful, it was also remarkable that there were cases which we had placed in our 'worst' scenario group where we considered that it would be highly unlikely that a parent would be engaged in the social work and protection process, but where by the end of the 6-months period a skilled social worker and sensitive procedures had resulted in active participation. There were other cases where it should have been very easy to work in partnership, but where either insensitive procedures or practice alienated parents and failed to involve them.

Working in partnership when the child is in care

We found that, in the one in five cases where the child was in care, strenuous attempts were made to work in partnership with the older children, although skills were sometimes lacking. However, those parents who were in conflict with the local authorities and whose child was away from home tended to receive a very poor service and few were involved in the work to any extent. The recent study by the Department of Health of adoption work in three local authorities confirms our impression that the service to parents whose children are to be placed permanently out of the home leaves much to be desired (DoH, 1993b). One explanation for this was to be found in some of the responses of parents. Social workers tended to offer counselling to 'come to terms with their loss', whereas at that stage parents were looking for negotiation and advocacy in order to continue to maintain a relationship with their child, even if they realised that he or she was unlikely to return to them. They still wished to be heard about the plans which were made for their child. It will be important to discover whether the requirement in the Act to consult them and give due consideration to their wishes and feelings will lead to greater parental involvement in such cases.

Conclusion

I conclude with some opinions and what I see as trends.

- One noticeable result of the emphasis on procedures, which is not inevitable but seems to be occurring in practice, is a tendency to lurch from meeting to meeting. Thus, Mary (whose case was referred to earlier) appreciated being involved in the planning and review meetings to discuss Jamie's future, and contrasted this favourably with her previous lack of involvement with the care system. However, she and Jamie lamented the lack of any time to talk with the social worker between these meetings. It seemed to us extremely worrying that there had been no social work contact with a young man who was so seriously depressed, which had allowed him to talk about his suicidal thoughts. Consultation and involvement in decision-making processes should be in addition to a skilled social work service based on relationships, and not instead of it. There are warnings here for the introduction of purchaser/provider arrangements which may result in the loss of a relationship-based service and increase the tendency to attempt to do everything in meetings which, however well conducted, are always going to be stressful events.

- Partnership principles at the stage of entry into the service seem to be rarely adhered to. No doubt this results from a lack of resources and a fear of, as so many workers put it, 'being swamped'. More attention should be given by solicitors, law centres and other advice agencies as well as social workers in intake or reception teams to helping children in need to claim their rights to a co-ordinated service under the Children Act. This will not necessarily involve a social worker, since most of those seeking the service are looking for practical help. Why, when under Community Care legislation adults can have an assessment based on need and a clear statement of services to be provided after consultation with them and their carers, can children and their families only have a service based on the assessment of risk? Services available under the provisions of the Children Act 1989 should be based on assessed need, with prioritisation according to the degree of impairment of health or development which is likely if services are not provided. When only risk of harm from parents or carers is taken into account in deciding about priorities, some highly needy children and families are precluded from receiving a service. At times when undertaking our research study it seemed that those who wanted a service and could use it were denied it, whilst those who didn't want a service and couldn't use it had it forced upon them. Not surprisingly in such circumstances, it was usually a far from effective service.

- Partnership is not possible in all cases, at all times, and may sometimes be inappropriate. But, attempts to work in partnership usually go alongside good practice to the benefit of children and parents. We saw very little indication in our 'Partnership in Child Protection' study that attempts to work in partnership with family members impeded the provision of an adequate service for the child. Where this did happen, it was because the worker did not recognise the importance of allocating different workers for the child who had been abused and for the abusing parent. Once this was recognised, the initial deficits in the service to the child were made good.

- The crucial components of practice which achieve family involvement are negotiation and advocacy skills. When these skills went alongside a value base which recognised the rights of parents and children to be involved, there was a higher likelihood that parents and children would be involved in the work and decisions, irrespective of the methods or therapeutic approaches used.

- There are advantages in the devolved budgets which come with Community Care policies in that they can offer greater flexibility of intervention. However, there is a danger in too much rigidity about who will be the main worker. Parents and children do not wish to be passed around like parcels, and relationship is still central to services which are perceived as helpful. In other words, family members must be consulted about who is the best person to offer a service, and whether a change of worker is appropriate. There were some cases where benefit resulted from a change of worker after the child protection conference, and others where this was deeply resented since the parents and child had come to trust the worker conducting the investigation and did not want to go through it all again with somebody new. Unnecessary changes of worker are not only resented by family members, but they are also not cost effective in that time must be spent by the new worker to make a relationship and overcome the resentment family members feel when a change is imposed upon them. Too many changes already result from resignations and career changes without increasing the numbers of workers involved for administrative convenience.

- Systems which artificially split 'purchasers' from 'providers' of services will be counter-productive if they do not ensure continuity of relationships between family members and the key worker or case manager. In child protection work 'purchaser' and 'provider' roles have to be held by the key worker who must have the power to make decisions and allocate resources, including the resource of her own time as a dependable and available professional presence. This does not, of course preclude the provision of additional specialist services with the key worker providing continuity, and indeed some of the work most valued by family members was provided by partnerships between family centre workers and area team key workers.

- There are signs that more work is being undertaken under Part III of the Act, without recourse to the courts. Central to this is a decision about 'co-operation'. Is the family likely to co-operate?; the reasonable parent test. But that requires a reasonable local authority test also; is the local authority willing to negotiate about the sort of services which might be seen as helpful? There is no room for the single method practitioner; 'it's either transactional analysis (or perhaps feminist group work or whatever else is the preference of that worker or manager) or nothing because that is what we do here' – approach. It was heartening to see that in a substantial minority of cases we studied the family members were given a choice of social work approaches or methods, and in a smaller number some choice about the social worker to be allocated to the case.

Despite the many obstacles resulting from lack of resources, (including training in the necessary skills such as negotiation and report and agreement writing), unhelpful policies and the degree of difficulty and complexity of many of the cases, our two studies provide evidence that some very hard-pressed social workers and agencies are working in partnership with families and children in some very unlikely cases. It is important to make sure that this current round of research findings helps us to learn from these practitioners and build their ways of working into training programmes. I am convinced from the cases I have studied over the last five years that, firstly, it will be better for children and their parents, and, secondly, it will be cost effective, if concerted attempts are made to involve family members in the design and provision of services and in the decision-making process. Negotiation at an early stage will, if nothing else, save a great deal of money on unnecessary court costs, and preserve more of the emotional energy of parents and of professional helpers working in partnership to achieve a better future for children in and out of care.

Notes

1. Children Act 1989 sections 20(6) and 22(4).
2. See the article by Lewis (1992) for a summary of the earlier research studies, and Thoburn et al. (1995) for the full account of our partnership in child protection study.

6 Working with children
Brynna Kroll

'Wisdom denotes the pursuing of the best ends by the best means'.
Francis Hutcheson (1694-1746) *'Inquiry into the Original of Our Ideas of Beauty and Virtue'* I:v

'Partnership' has become a very fashionable word in social work circles. Together with its companion 'empowerment' it has been liberally sprinkled upon the bumpy and often unyielding terrain we know as working with people in various kinds of difficulties. Rather like the application of peat and compost, these terms are seen to render the ground more accepting of growth. They also convey a number of illusions: that a partnership based on equality is possible and that power held by one party can be bestowed on another. I will be arguing that in relation to families in general and in relation to children in particular, these terms have to be examined purposefully if we are to understand what they really mean (if anything) and how some semblance of the philosophy behind them can be put into practice.

As with much social work jargon, these words have a tendency to make people who have to do unpleasant things to other people, sometimes against their will, feel better. They also enable practitioners to deny, at least for a time, the real power they hold over others. Thus, in the spirit of the Children Act, social workers form partnerships with parents who are, for example, mistreating their children, and empower them to take responsibility for their behaviour and their children's welfare. Various tasks and respective responsibilities are then set out in contracts or agreements, which all parties sign. All those concerned are clear that, in the context of this partnership, if parents do not keep their side of the bargain, there will be certain consequences. What happens if social workers fail to keep their side of the bargain is less clear. Already we can see the implicit inequality inherent in this process, although it involves a relationship between adults. How much greater the potential for abuse, then, when it comes to children.

Partnership, as defined by the Oxford English Dictionary, is 'an association of two or more persons for the carrying out of business of which they share the expense, profit and loss'. Clearly, this is unlikely ever to be applicable to child care work as we know it. The word 'partnership' is not in fact in the Act at all but it is apparent that many of its principles are informed by the notion of working with, rather than in opposition to, parents. As far as children are concerned, it has been argued that there is considerable evidence to suggest that partnership with children is not only a possibility but is positively advocated (Freeman, 1992). The fact that children's wishes and feelings should be sought and their views established, that they have the right to refuse examinations, that attention should be paid to children's culture, race, religion and language, and that sixteen and seventeen year olds can be accommodated against their parents' wishes, are all cited as examples of partnership in practice (op.cit.). This is stretching the definition of partnership somewhat; surely all that this reflects is good anti-discriminatory practice consistent with good social work, embracing, as it should, respect for the individual, recognition of need and difference and the right to be heard. As Freeman goes on to point out:

> The principle of partnership will not be easy to put into practice .... The emphasis on partnership, like that on parental responsibility, is in part an exercise in social engineering. As ever, it will be social workers who will take the blame if it does not work. (Freeman, 1992:25)

To view the use of partnership in the social work context as an exercise in social engineering perhaps goes to the heart of the matter. It is akin to the 'rule of optimism', where one sees what one wants to see and people become the people one wants them to become, doing the things one fondly hopes they can do (Parton, 1979). Parents do not assume parental responsibility because the law tells them to; neither do they work 'in partnership' – which, for many parents, amounts to sleeping with the enemy – because a government paper states that it would be a good idea. This concerns illusions of equality; it also concerns tensions between the welfare of the child and the rights of the parent. It was ever thus; legislation and terminology does not change the fact that some people are unable to care appropriately for their children and, as a consequence, someone else has to take action. This is the often unacceptable face of social work, the element of control and authority. Often what children and young people most need when things get desperate is someone who will take charge; they don't want a partner, they do not want to be empowered, they want a functioning adult who hears what they have to say, but is also able to make decisions. Partnership, in this context, is working together, but mindful that one participant is a grown-up and the other is not, and that there is a power differential. There is really no point in the invention of grown-ups, from a child's point of view, unless they can demonstrate a capacity to take charge and make things happen. As with any vulnerable group, this has implications. How then can we put these notions into practice?

The power imbalance between any adult and any child is

instantly apparent. Children are among the most oppressed members of society, overpowered – often literally and frequently metaphorically – by parents and by other grown-ups in their orbit. An hour in a busy supermarket or a playground demonstrates more clearly than anything the status accorded to children; we do not talk to anyone else with such disrespect and with such disregard for explanations and levels of understanding. We tell them to shut up, to stop asking 'why?', we threaten to kill them, throttle them or hit them ; sometimes we do actually hit them and then hit them again, when they imitate us by hitting someone else. We then wonder why some children behave as they do both to their parents and to others (Miller, 1987). How do workers address this power imbalance, enable a working alliance to be established, so that the child's wishes and feelings can be established as required by the Act? What do they need in terms of philosophy, knowledge base and skills, so that they can work effectively with children, aware of the differences, but equally aware of their right, as individuals, to be heard and understood? How can an approach be developed, based on the kind of partnership that makes sense , in this context? These are the questions I want to address, since I think they pose a number of dilemmas for practice.

Issues for practice

The Children Act clearly demands a great deal of workers in relation to children. The welfare checklist sets out the matters to which regard must be given, with a clear emphasis on establishing both the child's feelings and needs. This raises a number of issues.

- How do we talk to younger people? What about play as a way of communication? What do workers need in terms of skills and techniques?

- How do we clear our minds sufficiently to pay proper attention to the child without allowing other considerations to intrude (the next appointment, the court date, what parents/others have said about what the child thought/felt)?

- How do we make real contact with a child, create a safe place and establish a good enough relationship to encourage confidences?

- What can be achieved in the few sessions that are often all the time we get with a child? How do we make the most of this time?

- How can a focus be maintained, a framework for discussion be provided, while at the same time leaving room for the child's own contribution, so that there can be a non-directive element to the sessions?

- How can 'leading the witness' and 'contaminating the interaction' be avoided given the speed with which things often have to be done?

- How can the way the child makes the worker feel be used both to help parents become more aware of the child's predicament and to inform the assessment, the principal aim of the work?

All this requires making real contact with a child. Children's needs cannot be catered for by pouring resources into parents as though, by some magical process of osmosis, the child will automatically receive support at second hand. The ink is now dry on the contract made with the parents. What about the children?

Listening to Children

Children are a problem for many social workers; they are not at all sure what to do in relation to them and how appropriate child focused work might be accomplished. Despite the Children Act, social workers still spend little time with their younger clients. Sometimes they are seen, but not for long; sometimes they are seen but not heard. Demonstrable adherence to the Children Act 'welfare checklist', including establishing the child's views and wishes, is not accompanied by guidelines as to how establishing these should best be done. Workers who do feel it is important to offer children a service feel hampered by lack of time and expertise. Excuses and rationales for not having direct, meaningful contact with children abound. I suspect the real reasons are to do with the feelings engendered in workers by children who are having a difficult time, for whatever reason. Working with children is painful. It is often about loss, anger, rejection, neglect and sadness; it is also often about limited options and second rate solutions. It touches private life in tender places, it is unbearable and it makes us feel hopeless, helpless, sad and angry. Many workers admit to keeping children at a distance in an attempt to avoid feeling these feelings, to protect themselves from the pain, and to preserve a sense of competence (Kroll, 1994).

However, establishing children's views, their real feelings, as opposed to the views that parents wish them to express, is a tricky business. Like adults, children fantasise from time to time, do not always tell the truth, and may adapt the facts to suit their purpose. There is indeed a danger in placing too much weight on what children say. However this does not seem a reasonable argument for avoiding discussion or attempting to understand the child's experience. Canvassing a child's opinion does not automatically presuppose acting on it. It is possible, and indeed essential, to have sensitive, thoughtful, conversations with a child about their circumstances, their situation and the available options without handing them the power to decide their own fate. Clearly the type of situation that arose in a recently reported case (Phillips, 1993) is to be deplored. In that particular instance, a child felt forced, in the pressurising and intimidating atmosphere of the court environment, to choose between her parents, and then had her hard-wrung and hesitant preference acted upon without further investigation. This approach clearly distorts the ideal of ascertaining the wishes and feelings of the child and, while it may accord with the letter of the Act, it totally disregards its spirit.

The worker involved in that unfortunate case may well have believed that he/she was providing a child-centred service, because some time was spent with the child establishing her views and feelings. What is clearly demonstrated here is that it is not that simple. How might it be done differently? How might the task be achieved, while still keeping children at the centre of the work, with access to a real service which acknowledges not only their needs, but the complexities inherent in individual circumstances involving intense emotions, intimate relationships and different levels of awareness and understanding?

A 'starter kit' for practice

What I want to suggest is a way forward, a 'starter kit'[1] for this kind of work; some professional 'lego' that can be put together by workers, and that can be combined with their own individuality and expertise, to build a model for child-centred social work. This is the key to any real partnership.

This kit comprises four essential building blocks:

- A child-centred philosophy.

- A theoretical reservoir.

- A tool-bag of techniques.

- Access to appropriate training, supervision and support.

All four interlock with the Principles and Practice in Regulations and Guidance produced by the Department of Health (DoH, 1990) and that form the central core of the Children Act, and thus potentially provide the worker with the resources needed to do this work effectively.

The result is not a 'How To Do It' manual, a checklist in disguise, requiring nothing more than routine application for success. This would be impossible. This is a 'how to start thinking about it' guide, a professional synthesis, a set of principles, a range of complementary frameworks, akin to that provided by the authors of *Principles and Practice in Regulations and Guidance* and, un-ashamedly, I borrow their analogy:

> Principles are the colours on the social worker painter's palette. The range and quality of colour helps to produce a good painting but it is the painter's skill which makes or mars the picture. (DoH, 1990:17)

Understanding the principle is the first step; harnessing this to individual skills and applying this potent mixture differentially to individual clients is the art.

A child-centred philosophy

A child-centred philosophy sounds very laudable and grand, but what exactly does it mean? It starts, perhaps, with respect for children, with a belief in the value of child-centred work and a readiness to embrace the complexities and distress that this might involve on both a professional and a personal level. It is a way of placing children alongside adults as clients in their own right, as individuals who also need to have their say, as equals in terms of their entitlement, as people to be seen and heard. If a genuinely non-discriminatory service is to be provided by social work agencies, then children have to be added to the long list of groups vulnerable to misunderstanding, stereotyping and oppression. The Children Act, with its emphasis on ascertaining the wishes and feelings of the child, gives a clear message in relation to this issue, underlined by the Principle and Practice Guidance:

> Young people's wishes must be elicited and taken seriously. Even quite young children should be enabled to contribute to decisions about their lives in an age appropriate way. Learning to make a well informed choice is an important aspect of growing up and must involve more than just sitting in on reviews and conferences at which adults have all the power and make decisions. (DoH, 1990:12)

In the context of some social work agencies, it is apparent that certain approaches militate against children having any power since they may only be seen as part of the family system, rather than as individuals in their own right. Once again, it is important to emphasise that an individual approach does not mean the decision-making should be left in their hands – far from it – but rather that their views should contribute to the debate, and that their feelings about the experience should be known about. Implicit in this is that children are deserving of the respect, time, attention and thoughtfulness required to elicit their views, which, as the Guidance observes: '... involves direct, highly skilled and probably time consuming work with children especially if they are very young ....' (DoH, 1990:17).

In this context, as Freeman (1992) makes clear, a range of issues needs consideration. These relate to communication skills, objectivity, style of questioning and appropriateness of methods used. Children, like adults, have their own boundaries and their own time scale, their own ways of conveying their thoughts and feelings. A child-centred approach has to embrace and respect these differences. Acknowledging these is surely what something akin to partnership is about.

Getting in touch with one's own inner child can be a good way of beginning the process of putting oneself in the child client's shoes. It is a way of recalling what we knew, what we understood, what we thought of grown-ups and what we needed from them at different ages. This can often be a painful process, but elicits the kind of self-knowledge that enables us to know something important about the work being undertaken. It also enables the creation of a safe place where children can feel welcomed, prepared for and understood; the provision of what Winnicott (1971) has called 'holding', with the added dimension provided by Bion's notion of containment (1959;1962), where strong feelings can be explored and detoxified in the context of a dynamic relationship between child and worker.

A child-centred approach, however, cannot take place in a vacuum. Most children belong somewhere and to somebody, and child clients are all too aware of the implications of this. This is where the making of useful and open relationships with parents, the development of working partnerships so strongly advocated by the Children Act, comes in, despite the atmosphere of wariness and suspicion which often characterises the worker/parent relationship. The recognition of parents' needs as individuals has implications for the approach chosen. Clearly partnership is harder to achieve if parents feel coerced into working in a way that they find uncomfortable or stressful, and time must be taken to establish a foundation upon which a working relationship can be built. The danger is that, given that time is not infinite, choices have to be made about how much time is devoted to what. One obvious danger is that the children concerned get less of it than the adults. The time factor also has implications for the work done with children and how that is undertaken. I consider that a crucial aspect of the worker's role is to make it clear to parents why they want to see and speak to their children, and what they will not be saying as well as what they will be trying to achieve. The aim should be to enhance and facilitate communication between parents and their children, interpreting, if necessary, the needs and feelings of each to the other, and using the work with individuals to inform an understanding of the family system as a whole. The fear in the minds of parents, and sometimes workers too, is often that the worker will either compete with, or will be seen to be competing with, or replacing parents, if special time with children is sought. Openness, in the context of partnership, is clearly essential to alleviate such fears, as is the worker's capacity to look inside the self and explore the motives within.

All this takes time – time to be with people, time to allow them to tell their story, to enable them to discharge some of the pain, distress and anger that family difficulties bring, time to allow them to think about what has taken place and make sense of it, and time to talk to others and share impressions, as well as explore confusions and uncertainty. The amount of time taken needs to be considered in the context of both long and short term goals; a thorough assessment and a speedy decision are not always compatible, and the pace at which people are able to enter into a working partnership with a professional does not always accord with a court's timetable. It was after all a lack of thinking, breathing time that contributed to many of the tragedies revealed by the inquiries into the deaths of children returned home after having been received into care. Thinking time is crucial.

A theoretical reservoir

Now that a philosophy has been established, both a practical and a theoretical perspective need to be considered to provide frameworks for thought and understanding: a reservoir of ideas that can be drawn upon and used to make sense of the world of children, the things they do and the things they say.

On a practical level, relative size becomes important, in terms of getting on the same level as the child client rather than towering over them; tone of voice also needs to be considered. How do we talk to children? What voice do we need? How can we be authentic rather than patronising? What did we, as children, make of grown-ups who seemed to speak in one voice to other grown-ups and in another, several octaves higher, to us? An awareness of a child's time-scale and sense of time passing is essential, particularly when loss and change are realities; a week without contact between a small child and a parent can feel like a lifetime. Language needs to be both age-appropriate and sensitive to the way different words are used to mean different things, depending on background and culture.

We also need to know how children work, physically, cognitively, psychologically, and how to understand how they might feel through appropriate means of communication and interpretation. This involves putting together different but complimentary theories and frameworks: sets of windows through which the child's inner and outer world can be observed.

As a starting point, it is important to know what children should/should not be able to do or understand at different ages, and the kinds of developmental tasks with which they may be wrestling which might influence their fears and preoccupations. A working knowledge of child development on a physical level is essential, since this enables some assessment to be made about developmental delay or regression, both possible responses to emotional stress. It is also important to know about age-appropriate play and what a child might be expected to understand in terms of concepts and ideas. Both Sheridan (1968; 1992) and Fahlberg (1982) provide invaluable guidance in these areas: sufficiently specific and yet realistically general in terms of likely physical attainment.

Thinking about a child's cognitive and overall psychological development, from a range of standpoints, helps to build up a picture of the growing child moving through stages of development, each presenting its own set of hurdles and challenges which have to be overcome before the next stage can be entered (Piaget, 1969; Erikson, 1965; Freud, 1905). The task for the worker is to think about where the child might be according to the frameworks that make the most sense. They should decide what fits, and therefore what can be learned about where the child might be and how they are, in every sense. The important thing is to get an idea of what might be going on for the child on a number of different levels. It is also useful to reflect on the fact that chronological age and developmental age may be at odds, communicating something which may be significant.

Psychodynamic concepts, rooted in Kleinian and object relations theory provide a way of thinking about children's experience with reference to both their inner world and anxieties, as well as those related to the real world outside (Mitchell 1986). Outward manifestations, through stories, play and drawing, provide possible clues to inside feelings; an awareness of the importance and significance of transitional objects sheds light on a child's use of such objects to entrust an important part of the self to the worker. Being open to the way children make you feel often indicates something crucial about how they are feeling themselves. This information can enable real understanding and empathy to take place, and can assist in an increase in awareness between children and their parents. Kleinian theory, rather than being about stages of development as such, is about 'positions': fluid states of being, within which the individual oscillates throughout life. Although it could be argued that these positions, and the anxieties and defences that accompany them, are incompatible with more schematic, developmental frameworks, a mixture of these perspectives, depending on personal inclination, is a viable option.

A working knowledge of attachment theory and mourning

theory, as these relate to children, is essential. Children who come to the attention of child-centred agencies are likely to be experiencing problems related to attachment, or may be about to experience change, separation or loss. As Aldgate (1988) observes, it is very hard to understand the impact of separation without knowledge of attachment theory. By the same token, an awareness of the stages of mourning in children and how these may manifest themselves is invaluable (Jewett 1984)[2].

In this context, of course, the whole issue of interpretation becomes relevant, as does the way it can be used. I think that, in the first instance, interpretation is a silent activity undertaken for the benefit of the worker, to clarify thinking; it goes on in one's head and can be acted on. Telling anyone else about it is not always necessary, relevant or helpful. Having said that, there are times when interpretations can be usefully shared with children. There is risk involved, but if you are wrong, children are very quick to let you know. If you strike a chord with the child, something useful can come of it. The value of an interpretation is that it provides the worker with hunches and hypotheses about what might be going on, clues rather than definitive answers. These can then be presented to children as exactly what they are, clues and hunches; you may wonder if things are as you suspect, you may ponder, you may guess. Most things are open to a range of interpretations; this is not so much a quest for truth as an exploration. As a tool, it belongs on the voyage rather than at the destination.

At this point, then, the worker has developed a child-centred philosophy, a reservoir of theoretical knowledge from which to draw and an understanding, within this context, of what children at a certain age might know and understand, as well as what they can or should be able to do. Reflections on one's own memory, understanding and awareness at a similar age is an essential addition, provided of course that the worker is able to be the worker and the child simultaneously. The first two building blocks are now in place.

Communicating with children and the art of 'being'

How can the dialogue that now takes place between worker and child be facilitated? The first step is to clear the decks – sorting things out in your head so that you can give yourself over to the time with the child, without your previous appointment, your next appointment, your unwritten records, court dates and the fact that you have forgotten to buy anything for dinner getting in the way. The time can then actually be spent *with* the other person, rather than fighting off other preoccupations that clutter up the mind – your statutory powers, the deadline for your next report, the fact that you only have half an hour and you need all this information....

The second step is to develop the art of 'being' rather than 'doing' –
although clearly 'doing' at times is essential. This is the capacity in
workers to open themselves up to the experience of being with a
child (or an adult, for that matter) in a state that can perhaps best be
described as one of listening stillness, in which the urge to do, fix,
reassure, telephone and write things down is resisted. Instead, the
worker has to really be, so that the child's feelings can be known
about. 'Doing' will be necessary, but as a purposeful activity, rather
than as a defence; 'being' is an important quality to cultivate. This
is a central aspect of the kind of partnership that can be achieved
with a child, in which you can begin to know something about 'the
expense, profit and loss' inherent in that child's experience, even if
you cannot share it. Learning this particular skill, and developing it,
when there is such an emphasis on 'doing' is not easy. Space has to
made for it, and it needs to be supported as a valid activity,
underpinned by relevant training if necessary[3].

Once the state of 'being' has been achieved, consideration has to
be given to ways in which children communicate and how adults
can learn about this. Communicating with children requires the use
of play, drawing, and imaginative ideas that make talking about
painful and difficult subjects possible. Play, for children, represents
an expression of the unconscious with symbolic significance, rather
as free associations and dreams do for adults, and as such is a
valuable source of information (Klein, 1955). For play of any kind to
work, however, all participants have to feel comfortable with it.
Workers need to find their own way of being at ease with children,
as well as feeling comfortable with the idea of play as work, work
that worker and the child can do together. It is also important to
share the imaginative life of children. Retaining a belief in make-
believe, with a readiness to enter into children's fantasy games can
provide access to important fears and preoccupations. Children, of
course, go in and out of fantasy, often without warning; sometimes
we are not told that the fantasy has ended and we end up feeling
rather silly. Feeling silly is a small price to pay for being allowed
into someone's private world. Children's capacity for what Jewett
(1984) calls 'magical thinking' also needs to be kept in mind, both in
terms of children's capacity for omnipotence and in relation to a
belief in magical solutions to complex problems.

Techniques and ideas for communication with children are
numerous (Lieberman, 1979; Oaklander, 1978; Axline, 1964;
Aldgate and Simmons, 1988; Kroll, 1994). They are not definitive
and they cannot be used in every situation in the same way, since
the worker needs to make them her or his own. There is also a need
for time to try out, time for the child to engage in the activity. It is
clearly essential, when using games, role play, or any other
approach designed to evoke feelings, that there is enough time to
deal with what emerges from it. Games and techniques are valuable
in providing a safe way of making contact and creating potential

apertures through which inner thoughts and feelings might be glimpsed.

Managing the pain: training, support and supervision

Working with children is not easy. Training, support, supervision and a sense that expertise is valued are all essential. What do workers need in terms of training? What do they need from their colleagues, managers and agencies in order to enable this kind of work to be undertaken?

It would seem axiomatic to provide child development teaching to all students undertaking social work training at pre-qualifyng level, irrespective of their prospective specialism. This not only facilitates a grasp of how children work but also enables workers to respond to, understand and work with the child-within-the-adult, so often activated or resurrected by the traumatic events which bring people to the attention of social work agencies. Such teaching should ideally be reinforced by, and integrated within, a 'direct work with children and young people' sequence for those likely to be working with children at any professional level, or in any professional context. Combining various theoretical frameworks related to children in different age groups with experiential work and role play would enable students to gain awareness of their own feelings, and to enter the world of their child clients. A child study sequence, which provides the opportunity for a period of direct observation of children, should also form part of the generic first year Diploma in Social Work Training (DipSW), as indeed it already does in several social work departments[4].

At post-qualifying level, training has to address the continuing needs, on both a practical and an emotional level, of those who choose child-centred areas of practice. There is a considerable degree of insecurity among experienced social workers, who, faced with a child client, feel deskilled, and at sea (Kroll 1994). The model outlined for pre-qualifying training, in this context, could form the basis for a 'refresher' in relation to child development; theory harnessed to an experiential element, the skills associated with communicating with children, and case discussion would seem to be a sound place to start. Training, however, cannot take place in a vacuum. Once the process of exploration in this area begins it needs to be nurtured and supported through group discussion, case presentation seminars, debate and feedback. A climate needs to be provided in which difficult issues can be explored and discussed by people struggling with the same dilemmas. By this means, skills can be enhanced, expertise can be valued and professional development can be supported.

Back to basics?

I believe that agencies need to rethink what social work is all about
– fast. In responding to the chaos created by poverty, homelessness,
oppression of every kind, unemployment, rising crime, drug and
alcohol abuse, AIDS, the disintegration of 'the nuclear family', child
abuse in many forms, moral 'panics', and the increasing divorce
rate, there is a move towards devices that control and manage rather
than those which facilitate and encourage listening and exploring.
There is a tendency to over-simplify, often through the use of
worker-led or manager-led approaches that deny or ignore the
complex needs of people for whom the service was designed in the
first place. The thinking, feeling, contemplative and imaginative
social worker who wants to spend time making an assessment,
talking to clients, being uncertain and struggling with that feeling
is in danger of becoming the social work equivalent of the dinosaur.

Yet the Children Act demands such workers, requires just these
qualities and skills, if all the complex tasks identified are to be
accomplished. As a consequence, child-centred agencies and their
managers need to attend not only to case management but also to
practice, the encouragement of skills development, of openness
about the impact of the work, of further training, as well as the
celebration and validation of expertise.

Social work seems to have forgotten that people are its greatest
resource and that they need to be taken care of. To work with
children in need, in pain, in distress, in whatever context, and to
attend to them properly, the worker needs to be attended to as well.
Social workers with the commitment and training to work in the
way I have described need to be enabled to develop, and need to be
nourished, in order to survive. The social work tradition requires
people to be thoughtful, reflective, willing to learn and to grow, to
take risks, to be prepared to explore the child's world and to be able
to integrate the knowledge skills and values laid down by the
Children Act. To do all this, though, workers need help, when they
get stuck, from someone who knows what they are talking about.
Perhaps it is time for the return of the Senior Practitioner who gets
promoted on the basis of practice expertise and wisdom rather than
management ability.

My fear, however, is that social work will turn its face increasingly away from the child as an individual and continue to focus on
either the parents or the family system as a whole, because it is
easier. Forests will continue to be felled to provide more and more
checklists, assessment schedules and the ubiquitous contract,
unless the powers that be can be persuaded that there may be
another way. There is clearly no perfect way to do this work, but a
climate needs to be created in which different approaches can be
more thoughtfully combined, so that partnership with children,
without abnegating responsibility, can actually be attempted.

Room must be made for a short term therapeutic service in the context of a statutory task, so that valid assessments about children can be made which include the children themselves. In order to make the most of limited contact, the 'starter kit' provides a way forward, a fertile place in which individual practice can grow. Working with children in distress is far from easy. It is tempting to try to manage the complex nature of it by over-simplification, labelling, the use of mechanistic devices such as 'checklists'. Perhaps there is a need to stand back from this approach, and think more positively about ways of working with muddle, learning to make sense of the chaos and confusion of people's lives.

Practice and policy has to respond to the growing needs of families in trouble. When things go wrong, there are often many casualties, but the most vulnerable and powerless are children. If an appropriate assessment of their needs is to be made, their stories must be heard by someone who can bear to hear, and who has the appropriate tools to help them to make sense of it all. This is what partnership with children is all about.

Notes

1. For a fuller description of this see Kroll, (1994).
2. Claudia Jewett (1984) offers an invaluable analysis of the process of mourning in children – essential reading for anyone working with them.
3. I learned what 'being' really was – as well as how to observe properly – by undertaking child observation. Even when undertaken for a short period, this is an invaluable training and learning opportunity and I would argue that it should form part of every social worker's training, whether at pre-qualifying or post-qualifying level. If child observation is not possible, an awareness of the importance of thoughtful, listening stillness and the skills associated with it can be achieved through practice and application, in the context of appropriate professional support. See also Bick (1964), Miller et al. (1989) and Trowell and Miles (1991).
4. Inclusion of such a sequence would square well with the renewed emphasis in social work education on observation skills and adopting a non-judgemental stance in relation to individuals, as well as developing a capacity to 'be' rather than to 'do' – all skills which can be transferred to a wide range of other areas of practice. From my own experience of child study seminars at Diploma of Social Work level, I am aware of how hard it is for students to stop and think about whose needs they are really meeting when they leap into action. The sequence enables them to dig deep in to their own feelings of helplessness, sorrow and smallness, faced with the magnitude of the experiences they have to encounter.

7 Tri-partnership: statutory, voluntary, and private partnerships

Robin Solomon

The idea of partnership grew out of the 1989 Children Act as a result of an ideology that purported to be about the equalisation of power and responsibility for children between the state and parents. No one, right or left, could fault it at the time. Professionals from all arenas supported the principle, with lesser or greater degrees of enthusiasm and scepticism, and waited for The Act to change inequity which for years had surrounded the child care system.

In another arena of social care, we were assured that separate but unconnected legislation for adult service users, the elderly, the mentally ill and the disabled, was about to change the way social services were delivered. Like partnership under the Children Act, the Community Care Act was about consumer choice, equity, and equalisation of power. Not since Seebohm have we seen a bigger reorganisation of structures and systems for the delivery of care services.

The idea that the two statutes created programmes of change that could be discretely administered is in hindsight ludicrous. A department charged with the delivery of social care services from the cradle to the grave (comprehensive or residual), cannot reorganise its structure and philosophy of service delivery for the adult division without by extension redefining its services for children. Even without planned change, the ripple effect of organisational restructuring ensured the total revision of childcare services. Departments that were busy managing packages of care and buying services from voluntary agencies and private providers for adults, were only a glance away from using the same model for child care services.

In many local authorities, social workers were reconstructed to become care managers. This moved them away from being direct service providers to becoming purchasers of care services. In some local authorities this has progressed to the point of planned closure of, for example, residential/fostering and therapeutic services and into the setting up of firms or trusts that take on responsibility for providing these services. While in most boroughs these services are still at present part of the statutory sector, in some boroughs, these services are either being readied for a transition to independent status, put out to tender, or simply becoming redundant with a view to using the voluntary and private sector for almost all direct services.

In the area of child protection there has been the most resistance to embracing this new structure but that too is changing. In fact the pace of change is so frenetic, and the extent to which this change is being implemented is so varied across the U.K., that any attempt to write about it and capture an overall picture at this moment in time is practically impossible. A number of counties having adopted the model quickly are in the process of reconsidering. Others are still trying desperately to catch up.

Large voluntary agencies are undertaking research, or plan to, in order to evaluate their positions in these new models. I am therefore not undertaking to write a researched analysis about the success or failure of the partnership between the sectors. My aim is more modest: to examine the new model that is evolving in child care services and the partnership between the voluntary, private and statutory sectors within that model. I hope to present the reader with questions that must be asked if an analysis is to be undertaken. In order to explore this it will be important to look at three main issues:

- Whether partnership is consistent with a purchaser/provider model.

- Whether there is a distinct difference between child protection and other child care services.

- Whether it is therapeutically viable to split care and control.

Social Services cost money. Two main questions arise out of this. One is, where is the point of payment? The other is, who pays? Let us look at the first question. Payment for services can be made in either of two ways: at source or at the point of delivery. In the first case, payment is made by the taxpayer who contributes through taxes to the running of universal services. In the second, payment is made for the receipt of a service and at the point where the service has been provided. This method requires detailed costing and the identification of the payee.

The welfare state philosophy has always endorsed payment at source. Duties and responsibilities relating to levels and kinds of services have been set down by statute, custom and practice, and have been influenced by the outcome of local elections, leading to geographical variances. In its simplest sense, the aim was to see how much the provision of those services would cost in human and material terms and to ensure the service had enough funds to cover that cost. As far as the identity of the payer is concerned, payment was made by the taxable population. It was collected either through

central government taxes distributed to local authorities through
grants, or by local taxes levied through rates/community charges set
to meet the budget allocated to provide the agreed services. This
model has been criticised on the ground that little attention was
paid to the cost of each element of the service and, therefore, there
was no incentive to ensure the most cost-effective service.

The market economy model of social care is that a service is paid
for at point of delivery. Each aspect of the service is costed very
specifically with the intention of identifying areas for cost cutting
or greater savings. This is done with the aim of presenting either
the lowest running costs, if the service has to be sold to the
taxpayer, or the lowest bid for provision of a service, if it needs to
be sold at the point of delivery. Service provision could also be
opened up to the market place and aspects of social work services
supplied by agencies (voluntary and private) which could be
bought by the local authority. The underlying premise of this model
is that clear costing and competition would lead to lower costs of
service delivery. It is also assumed that an emphasis on precision
will clarify the thinking behind services and the planning for those
services, thus improving the quality of care.

But what of the second question? Who pays in a market economy
model of social care? Well, for those services still mandated by
statute, it is still the responsibility of the state to pay for the
services. This can be done with either of two models. As has been
done within the welfare state model, the local authority can be both
the payee and the service-provider. Put crudely, it pays itself at the
point of service delivery, thus ensuring that the cost of each service
is clearly identified and the local authority is made accountable for
each item on which it spends its funds. It is also the intention that,
mindful of its need to pay for each aspect of its provision, it will
provide only what is needed and nothing superfluous, as well as
being made aware of the cost of each service.

The alternative is to pay someone else for the delivery of a service
and therefore become in essence, the purchaser of that service. As a
prudent purchaser mindful of its taxpayers' money the local
authority is expected to shop around for the lowest costing services,
while retaining ethical and professional concern about the level of
quality. Its choice is either to compete with its own provision of
those services or to stop providing services and use its now larger
budget to pay for all of those services externally.

It is also prudent to anticipate that once services are so
specifically costed, it is only a short move to the expectation that the
user is also the purchaser, whereas now the purchaser is the local
authority/care manager and the consumer is the client. Thus
individuals buy their own care services. Whereas previously,
although there has always been a private mental health service, a
private children's service and private provision for the elderly, this
was always a small and elite service and the majority of services

were still universal. Now we are seeing elderly clients buy home helps, meals on wheels and residential care. While it can be argued that there is value in individuals buying their services, this arrangement lends itself easily to tiers of service depending on ability to pay for better quality services.

The move to this model of service provision for adult services has been mandated by community care legislation. There is as yet no national picture emerging as to the prevalence of this model permeating children's services, but it is clear that to a greater or lesser degree this conceptual structure is emerging in an increasing number of localities. Some, which I will go on to look at in greater detail, have fervently embraced this structure and see it as a way towards increasing quality of service while lowering expenditure. Others have been forced into this model through external pressures, and yet others are consciously resisting it through a commitment to maintaining a welfare state structure of service delivery. Some have not had the opportunity to fully consider their options or make to choices, as resource cuts have kept their attention elsewhere, and as such they still retain their existing structure.

A new structure of this nature must inevitably have an impact on the relationship between the voluntary and statutory sector. The idea of 'partnership' between these sectors in child care is in reality not a new one. There has always been a place for the voluntary sector in the provision of residential facilities, such as Barnardo's, N.C.H. Action for Children, Save the Children, and even smaller organisations like The Royal Philanthropic. While it was never called partnership, local authorities have always been using, and have, in many instances, been dependent upon the provision of certain types of care and service in the voluntary sector. This has meant paying for a place for an individual child or a service provided to an individual child or family. Use of these services has varied over time and place. There have been differences with regard to the quality of service provided, the location of the voluntary agency and its service, the ideology and practice wisdom at the time when a decision was made to approve or reject the use of 'out of authority' placements or the payment for external provision of services and resources.

Another area of children's service historically identified with voluntary agencies has been adoption (and from time to time fostering) services. While most authorities developed and ran their own adoption and fostering sections, some relied in total, and many in part, upon the national networks available through such voluntary organisations as B.A.A.F. or the Catholic Children's Society. For those authorities with well-developed fostering and adoption services, the roles and responsibilities of workers in the voluntary agency and the local authority were often blurred or overlapping. Certainly there were no formal 'contracts' between the two.

Throughout the late seventies and eighties, a new connection emerged. Jointly run and funded projects began to become more commonplace. Thus New Black Families, a joint family finding agency run between Independent Adoption Service and Lambeth Council was a progressive coming together of expertise and resources around an identified need. Leaving care projects, run by the Royal Philanthropic Society and Wandsworth Council, pooled and developed residential and support services for young care leavers.

So, the Children Act 1989 did not introduce the idea of partnership between the voluntary and statutory sectors as some have implied, but rather formalised these relationships, and then only in respect of the accommodation of children,[1] or specifically in relation to the NSPCC and child protection.[2] It appears, if one puts it in the context of the ideology of the Act as a whole, merely to have attempted to raise the status of voluntary agencies, or more specifically, to give them more power in relation to local authorities by breaking up the monopoly that they had held.

Two things, however, have changed drastically in this area; more, it appears, due to the community care purchaser/provider structure and the surrounding ideology, than to the Children Act itself. The first is the emergence of voluntary and private agencies and private individuals in the provision of what could be identified as field services, formerly almost the exclusive domain of local authorities. This has very specific implications in the field of child protection, but I will address those later.

The second change has been in the nature of the service that is being provided and in the use of contracts, or 'service agreements', to regulate the relationship between these sectors. Two models of 'service agreements' are emerging. One type is entered into at the point of purchasing a service for an individual. For example, an area locality (now with its own budget) assesses the needs of Lesley Smith aged 8. It is agreed that she needs to be accommodated, with the consent of her parents, for 8 weeks. It is agreed that because of her specific needs, a residential unit offering respite care for children with her particular difficulty would be the most appropriate place. There is one such unit, run by a voluntary agency, and so a service agreement is drawn up, identifying what the voluntary agency will offer, how much each aspect of its service costs, and who will be responsible for its overall implementation. The local authority (the purchaser) agrees to pay a fee for this service for this individual (the consumer), as well as to identify what responsibilities the locality has in relation to this placement, and by whom and how they will be met. The service agreement is the contract for the completion of these services and the agreement of a price. This is not so vastly different from previous out of authority placements. The difference is the specificity of task, and the breakdown of cost.

The other type of service agreements is perhaps less familiar. The local authority 'sub-unit' which is responsible for purchasing services (this could be as a consequence of geographic area or expertise), designs an agreement with a private or voluntary agency to provide a specific number of services for an agreed price. So for example, a voluntary agency which runs a family resource centre can be approached to provide a specified number of assessments per year at a fixed cost, thus agreeing a price per assessment as long as a set number of referrals is made. Alternatively, a lump sum grant can be made to the voluntary organisation as a contribution towards fixed costs (such as an extra post or capital expenses related to the set activity), under agreed guidelines guaranteeing that a specific volume or specific types of work will be allocated during a set period of time.

The core question that this model poses, as it unfolds, is who in the negotiating process has more power? It must be asked who makes decisions and how are these arrived at, whether these service level agreements actually constitute partnerships, or whether partnership is impossible in a model which necessitates the buying and selling of human services.

The model also highlights two other major issues concerning the relationship between the statutory and voluntary sector. Historically, the voluntary sector has played an important role in the development of new and creative services. Without the constraints of statute, voluntary bodies have been able to initiate new programmes and experiment with new methodology. They have also been, at times, the providers of services for client groups not recognised under statute. For example, culturally specific services or services for oppressed groups in society have often emerged through the voluntary sector by means of community projects responding to need. With a structure of service level agreements, the voluntary sector is now more obligated to provide service packages that are defined by the purchasing sector. If that purchaser is not interested in these services they will not be purchased or funded. Potentially, unless the voluntary sector can be financed in other ways, the nature of their projects and the client groups identified by their projects will become defined by the purchasing authority. On the other hand, if there is an identified need which is not being met by the statutory agency, the voluntary agency, with the help of pressure groups, can potentially use partnership arrangements as a way of ensuring the purchasing of specialised services by the statutory agency from the voluntary sector if the statutory agency cannot provide those services directly.

The market model is based on the buying and selling of objects. The price of a car or computer, say, depends upon wages levels, technology and brand marketing as well as quality and scarcity (supply and demand) of product. The question to which we all need to return is whether the market model of costing human services, promotes improved quality. Who is the assessor of that standard:

the user or the purchaser? In most instances in social services, these two are not the same. This is where the market model of welfare services differs from the market model that applies to commercial trade in objects. And in the case of child protection, there can be even further debate about the assessment of quality since the user might be seen as the purchaser, the child or the parent.

It is in the area of·child protection that we can perhaps see most clearly where some of the advantages as well as the tensions lie. Perhaps it is because previously, child protection was the sole preserve of the statutory sector and therefore one of the few arenas of child care where, with the exception of the N.S.P.C.C., 'partner-ship' with the voluntary sector has not evolved gradually and naturally. The starkness of the change raises all the inherent dilemmas.

Let us follow a fictitious case through this system as the basis for thinking about the concept of partnership between the agencies involved.

Someone telephones the social services with a referral about Johnny. This phone call is answered by the advisory officer, (or other title-holder) who by profession can be either qualified or unqualified, but in many areas is now unqualified. This person directs the referral to the appropriate location in the service; in this instance, to a case manager for child care. The case manager works in a locality team. Colleagues are often care managers for adult services, and although line managers might have a background in child care, often they have backgrounds in other specialisms. The case manager does the initial screening which usually includes checks with the relevant agencies and registers. If it is considered necessary, the case manager might do an initial visit in an emergency referral. Sometimes, however, even this initial visit is allocated to the provider team depending on circumstances and resources. The job of the case manager then is to organise a planning or strategy meeting and to commission a s47 investigation or a risk assessment. Alternatively, a case manager might provide an explanation for a decision that there should be no further action.

The comprehensive risk assessment is 'purchased' by the case manager and can be commissioned from the provider team (in-house statutory section), a family centre (which could be in-house statutory, external voluntary, or jointly funded and/or run agency), or by an 'independent' agency, (meaning a voluntary agency outside the statutory sector and the health service and not a private individual or group of individuals set up as a private provider). The cost of this assessment service is set by internal forces (in the case of in-house statutory providers), market forces (if an independent agency or individual is competing for the contract) or a combin-ation (depending on government grants or, in the case of the voluntary agencies, their charity budgets). Clearly, there is not necessarily 'a level playing field'.

The results of the comprehensive assessment by a provider are brought before the child protection conference to ascertain the level of risk. Protection plans, if needed, must be agreed, and part of the conference's responsibility is to decide what care plan will be safe enough, and which provider offers the best service to meet this plan. Different aspects of the plan, of course, can be distributed amongst various providers.

Let us look again at Johnny. It is agreed in the conference that following a full assessment of need and risk, the following services are needed:

- Someone to work therapeutically with Johnny and to make an ongoing assessment of progress.

- Someone to work with the parents around parenting skills, their relationship and their individual needs.

- A full-time school assistant to help Johnny in class because his trauma has affected his schooling and it is thought that he might have special educational needs.

- A temporary family placement where Johnny can be safe while some of the initial work is being undertaken.

- A family centre or equivalent for supervised contact between Johnny and his parents.

These various services can be provided in numerous ways. In the 'old model' of welfare state services, all, or most of these services could be provided by the local authority social services. Johnny's family would have a social worker who would both manage his case and build up a relationship with the family. S/he would use in-house teams to locate a foster parent, and either that social worker and/or the link worker for the family would visit him there. Simultaneously, that same worker would work with Johnny directly and get to know him, with the result that the worker would become a familiar and, theoretically, trusted adult. The same worker would also work with the parent/parents and, according to the dominant practice in the 1970s and 1980s, would develop a relationship with them. This practice was superseded by the use of contracts in the 1980s and 1990s but the worker would continue to be responsible for ensuring that contact visits were taking place in designated locations (often in-house but more recently external locations). Education authority work was done by referring children for assessment by a different service, and this involved a good deal of good-will and informal negotiation. The family centre (a relatively new concept preceded by the idea of nursery attendance) would be run by a local authority or, where the provision of that service was available in the locality by a voluntary agency, that would often be identified. A general sum would be paid for a placement in that agency or, in a small number of cases, 'free' places were provided because the agency saw its brief as being simply to provide such services.

Let us look at this same package under the new market economy model. The case manager oversees the case. S/he might have little or no direct contact with Johnny or his parents. S/he has no direct therapeutic role and is not concerned with developing a relationship with family members. S/he needs, however, to be very knowledgeable about what those aspects of the work entail, otherwise s/he cannot assess which available package is best. S/he will need to contact various possible providers, and like a careful consumer, study the different services on offer, the quality of those services, the detail of what they include, and of course, the price of each aspect of that service. S/he would then need to identify the provider who would supply the 'best deal', meaning, ideally, the best quality care at the best possible price. The question that remains to be discussed is whether there are any factors that influence how that decision is taken and what happens if the best quality of care is not at the lowest price.

In the case of Johnny, s/he would need to locate the following:–

- Someone to work therapeutically with Johnny and to make an ongoing assessment of progress. This could be a private individual therapist; a psychologist from an N.H.S. trust; a specialist from an N.S.P.C.C. unit in the area; or a named social worker in the in-house purchasing team with the necessary expertise and training.

- Someone to work with the parents around parenting skills, their relationship and their individual needs. This, like the person or people referred to above, could come from a similar variety of places, including smaller, voluntary agencies such as Relate.

- A full-time school assistant to help Johnny in class because his trauma has affected his schooling and it is thought that he might have special educational needs. This service must be bought from the relevant education authority, or, at least, negotiated with them to allow someone else, separately paid, to assume that role. This could also necessitate a payment to an educational psychologist for assessment, either separately, or as part of the bill presented by the education authority.

- A temporary family placement where Johnny can be safe while some of the initial work is being undertaken. This is the most urgent task. If the local authority concerned still has an in-house fostering section (which would be one of the service teams) then it would provide the service. The locality team, don't forget, will need to purchase this service from the service team, thus moving money from one in-house budget to another. The service will have to have been costed into unit costs to ensure it is giving value for money.

Alternatively, the local authority may not have a service team providing fostering services. This is now starting to happen in a small number of local authorities, where their fostering services are becoming either business unit subsections of the local authority (trust status) or becoming private organisations. In some instances, local authorities are having to 'buy' families from voluntary agencies. These agencies may have always worked in this way, but on a more limited scale; most social services departments had internal fostering teams and only bought out as a last resort for children with special needs or for specific reasons.

• A family centre or equivalent for supervised contact between Johnny and his parents. This could be a family centre run solely by the local authority (the current trend is to turn nurseries into family centres); or a voluntary organisation which runs a family centre in a geographic area; or, more commonly, one which is run by a voluntary agency but funded by the local authority and, therefore, a partnership agency. It is also not unheard of to find private family centres emerging in this climate.

The case manager is responsible for finding these services and presenting to the child protection conference the range of possible services. The conference then decides which packages should be purchased in order to provide a 'safe enough' care plan. It is then their responsibility to monitor those services and to ensure that they are actually being provided and that what is being provided is what was agreed in a service agreement.

Let us look at one of these service agreements in more detail and consider whether this model in fact constitutes partnership between the voluntary and statutory sector. As I have stated earlier in this chapter, there are three levels of service agreements. The first is the agreement between purchaser and provider over the service provided for an individual child or family, such as one agreed for Johnny and his parents above. The others are about providing a set number of such services at a specified cost per service or in fact running a service for the use of the purchasing authority.

Let us consider the first type. Johnny is in need of therapeutic services to help him deal with the trauma of abuse and separation. The in-house provider team cannot provide this service any longer due to staff shortages and a limited post-qualification training budget. A fictitious voluntary agency (for simplicity let us call it Post Abuse Counselling Service, or P.A.C.S.) is approached. Its workers say that, from the details of the assessment, they believe that Johnny is in need of six months of fortnightly sessions with a specialist counsellor. They feel that given their expertise in this specialist field of abuse, they can anticipate that for a child his age and with abuse of the nature specified, he would benefit from that time. A fee for six months' counselling is calculated, based on their running costs such as salaries, capital expenses, administration and their income, including grants from the government, from charity foundations and from individual donations.

There is also a new private agency opening in the local area called Children's Counselling Services Ltd. (C.C.S.Ltd.) owned and run by an ex-child psychotherapist from the N.H.S., one ex-guardian ad litem, and two ex-social workers with MAs in counselling. Because they are trying to interest the local authority in their service, they are offering a very low rate. They think Johnny needs nine months to a year of counselling but will charge a relatively small sum for the entire service. In future they are planning to charge by the session.

In this instance, what does partnership actually mean, and who is in partnership with whom? Presumably, the purchasing arm of the statutory agency will be in partnership with one of these other agencies. Certainly we are not talking here about a partnership between the statutory agency and Johnny, or the voluntary or private agency and Johnny (see Kroll in this volume). Are we then talking about a partnership between the parent and the provider agency? What if they do not want Johnny to receive such service? Or is there a partnership between the purchasing agency and the parents? But what if the parents want to go to C.C.S. Ltd. and the local authority workers opt to purchase the service from P.A.C.S. because they know its work is good and have heard through their networks that C.C.S. Ltd. has not provided adequate services in two other cases?

Presumably, partnership with the voluntary and private sectors was always meant to be about statutory agencies working together with those sectors in order to provide the best service for children and families and to offer the widest possibile consumer choice. But who is the consumer? Clearly, in child protection (and I would suggest in many statutory child-care services) the consumer is the purchasing arm of the local authority and not the family or child. The obligation under the Children Act to act in the best interest of the child, and as consumer to act on behalf of the child, could, I suggest, be in conflict with the obligation to act as a prudent consumer on behalf of the tax-payer. Thus the concept of partnership from the perspective of the statutory agency (and presumably the client) cannot be kept entirely separate from the purchaser ideology permeating social services departmental structures under community care legislation.

Viewed from the other side, how much 'in partnership' does the voluntary agency feel? If we return to the case of Johnny we can soon identify some of the dilemmas of the voluntary or private agency. The P.A.C.S. has said, based on its years of expertise that it will take six months to work with Johnny. What if the case manager said that, in her opinion, Johnny only needed three months of services. Or that, in her opinion, service should consist of family therapy sessions, not individual play therapy sessions with Johnny as the P.A.C.S. had suggested. What power does the voluntary agency in this instance have to negotiate these terms? At the moment, in the case of the large and well-known voluntary sector organisations, their status and expertise help them to maintain a negotiating position; if this case manager does not want to purchase their service, many others will. Likewise, they could 'undercut' smaller agencies because of their already established structures, larger budgets in some instances, and capacity to take bigger 'business risks'. In these instances, there might well be enough power on both sides to warrant the use of the term partnership. The question arises whether this balance of power would exist in the case of smaller private or smaller voluntary agencies. It might in the event that the service required is scarce. It is the responsibility of the case manager to ensure that the service is provided. If the provider refuses to provide the service as requested, there might be nowhere else that the service can be found. If, after shopping around, the case manager finds that there is no other service available, the provider may now be in the position where it has the power to decide on the cost and the content of the service. As in-house service provision has been reduced or abolished in many local authorities, local voluntary agencies or private providers are gaining a monopoly over services in place of the local authority monopoly which had led to the whole move to consumer choice and partnership.

The second level of service provision I referred to was the multi-unit service contract. Under this arrangement, the provider under-takes to provide a certain amount of a specified service at a set cost as long as the purchasers agree to purchase that amount of that service in that period of time. Thus, the local authority could purchase from the P.A.C.S. a service level agreement undertaking to provide 25 places for therapeutic services for abused children during the year. Johnny could be one of those 25. The maximum/ minimum service provision must be agreed in the service level agreement so that no one case manager can expect a care package from that agency beyond/below the agreed limit of service. This gives the voluntary agency some power to define what it provides because the local authority is dependent on it for a set number of places and has agreed to pay for the services in bulk. On the other hand, the local authority still maintains some power, because it can refuse to take up the bulk service if it is not to a particular standard; the agency is often dependent upon this money and could not afford to risk losing the contract.

Ideally this mutuality could be called a partnership and it might perhaps generate a high level of mutual monitoring, regulation and creative development. In reality, I believe, we are seeing in some instances a phenomenon which could be termed 'passing the buck'. Large groups of clients are being allocated as part of a bulk package because the agreement necessitates this, rather than as a response to their particular assessed need. Likewise, the voluntary agencies are at risk of being given inappropriate work as part of the contract package yet to return the client would be to breach the service agreement and to risk losing the funding.

This reliance by the service purchaser on the terms of the agreement enables it, effectively, to 'pass the buck'. Passing the buck is the art of allocation of work to external agencies and so to conserve in-house human resources. It is the passing of responsibility from one agency to another agency (or from one section of a large authority to another) to protect the worker from accountability for the quality of the service provided. So whereas the ideal is to exploit the partnership potential of these service agreements, the reality could be experienced as contradictory to partnership as a means of protection from external pressures on resources (both financial and human).

This leads me to my third area of concern: the question whether there is therapeutic sense in the splitting of care and control functions. Whilst we tend to discuss the viability of partnership as social policy, it is crucial from a social work perspective to think about this concept therapeutically as well. In order to do this it is necessary to consider Isabel Menzies'[3] work on institutional defences. Her seminal work, *The Functioning of Social Systems as a Defence Against Anxiety*, examines hospitals and considers how the structure of the organisation itself not only reflects the interpersonal and intrapsychic dynamics, but more importantly, perpetuates those dynamics. She demonstrates how structure is designed as a response to process while process is crucially defined by structure. She endorses the view that:

> Social institutions arise through the efforts of human beings to satisfy their needs, but ... social institutions then become external realities comparatively independent of individuals which affect the structure of the individual. (Menzies, 1970:34)

She goes on to explain that:

> nurses are confronted with the threat and the reality of suffering and death as few lay people are. Their work involves carrying out tasks which, by ordinary standards, are distasteful, disgusting and frightening .... The work situation arouses very strong and mixed feelings in the nurse: pity, compassion, and love; guilt and anxiety; hatred and resentment of the patients who arouse these strong feelings (Menzies, 1970:5)

She goes on to say that 'by the nature of her profession the nurse is at considerable risk of being flooded by intense and unmanageable anxiety' (Menzies, 1970:9). Her work uses psychoanalytic theory (Klein, Fenichel, Bion) to explain the phenomenon of projecting that anxiety into the external reality of the structure of the system that contains it. She describes a number of systemic phenomena which she believes are a direct result of this projective and introjective process. Some of these are:

- Splitting up the nurse-patient relationship (Menzies, 1970:11).

- Detachment and denial of feelings (Menzies, 1970:13).

- The attempt to eliminate decisions by ritual task performance (Menzies, 1970:14).

- Collusive social redistribution of responsibility and irresponsibility (Menzies, 1970:16).

- Purposeful obscurity in the formal distribution of responsibility (Menzies, 1970:18).

- The reduction of the impact of responsibility by delegation to superiors (Menzies, 1970:19).

If one considers current child-care social work, and particularly child protection, as tasks which 'by ordinary standards are distasteful, disgusting and frightening', as Menzies says, we can begin to look at the new restructuring and division of tasks and responsibilities in the context of her observations of hospital structures. If one thinks of the anxiety of the nurse/social worker as dependent on the closeness of her relationship with the patient/client, the closer the relationship the more intense the anxiety. Thus anything that can distance the worker from the client will be functional to her self-protection. In child care this has been demonstrated by the division of tasks between professionals, between workers in the same profession, and between agencies.

Likewise, Menzies describes decision-making by means of ritualised task-performance as a method of managing anxiety. She explains that decision-making necessitates uncertainty and un-knowingness (Menzies, 1970:14). This unknowingness stimulates anxiety, particularly if the decisions are as life-threatening or long-ranging as child-care decisions often are. To avoid anxiety, the decision-making must be diversified amongst many and removed from individuals. A ritualistic response to decision-making helps to distance individuals from the decision. The multi-disciplinary case conference might be understood in these terms. Menzies mentions a collusive social redistribution of responsibility and irresponsibility. What she describes is the phenomenon whereby nurses project qualities of responsibility and irresponsibility upward or downward. This is not a conscious process but a collective defence based on a collusive system of splitting, denial and projection.

Projection is an individual defence mechanism which occurs in human development when anxiety is so unbearable to the infant (and later adult personality) that parts of the self are split off and projected onto outside objects/people. In later life the more distant and without features the external object, the more susceptible it is to projections. The phenomenon of splitting (stemming from infancy when the child can't hold the experience of good and bad carer in the same person) is when all the good bits or all the bad bits get projected into different objects.[4]

Each nurse tends to split off aspects of herself from her conscious personality and to project them onto other nurses. Her irresponsible impulses which she fears she cannot control are attributed to her juniors. Her painfully severe attitude to these impulses and burdensome sense of responsibility are attributed to her seniors. It is also noted that additional protection from individual responsibility (and uncertainty) is gained by ensuring that the boundaries of roles are very obscure, especially at senior levels. The more complex the role distribution the easier it is to evade definition and personal responsibility.

This research sheds a great deal of light on some of the current tensions and the potential pitfalls of partnership between different agencies. By way of introducing this idea I would like to share a personal anecdote. I would also like to remind readers that the market economy model of social care introduced in the United Kingdom is not a unique innovation. It has been the major service delivery policy in North America since the inception of social services. There has also been a tradition of charity/voluntary services in North America and, therefore, this tri-partite system is well established. While acknowledging a different political history, it is important to note that the USA is in the throes of re-evaluating its market economy model of health-care provision because of the astronomical cost and the ever-increasing numbers of the population who have no access to private health-care for that reason.

In 1979, I moved to London from New York where I had done my social work training[5] which focused on therapeutic interventions. While in New York I worked in a clinic which offered a range of direct services to children and families. I was very conscious of the nature of therapeutic relationships and the relevance of transference and countertransference[6]. Likewise I was alert to defence mechanisms such as projection and splitting. Yet when I began my work in a social services department in an inner London borough, I was in for a rude awakening.

One of my clearest memories is of a young woman, H, with whom I was working. She was 16 and in care because of a breakdown in communication between herself and her mother. Her mother felt she was out of control. As I developed a relationship with her, and that was difficult due to her volatile nature and the rebellious developmental stage she was in, I was mindful of the transference and countertransference issues. Certainly for H, I represented her mother, and much of my work as I then understood it, was to interpret that material therapeutically. What was new to me, and struck me forcibly one memorable day in the office, was that in fact, my representing her mother was not solely a transferential issue as I had been trained to understand, but rather, as placing me in 'loco parentis' on behalf of the local authority. I was acting as her 'mother', or at least, as someone with a degree of legal responsibility. Thus her fury with me when I refused her yet another clothing grant for a party dress was not a manifestation of behaviour towards a transferential figure of authority, but was in fact fury at me, Robin, for making a practical and material decision affecting her. For her, I was not only symbolically her mother, I was acting as if I were in fact her mother.

After my initial shock at this revelation, and a terrible crisis of confidence in my ability, I reconsidered my role as a social worker in Britain. I was not only a therapeutic carer, but also a legally responsible carer, and, depending on the ideological/legislative remit at the time, I could also be, to a lesser or greater degree, an agent of social control. I not only had perceived power but I also had real power, manifested in the giving and withholding of material goods. Whereas in New York I had been the therapist, and legal and practical decisions were made by the state agencies, here in Britain I was both therapist and legal guardian.

What was wonderful about this revelation to me was that I discovered the value of being both the carer and the controller, the therapist and the guardian, the good guy and the bad guy embodied in the same worker. When working with abused children at least, this had the benefit of offering a truly 'reparenting' experience to a child (or the needy child within the parent). That I held this position, I believe, was one of the reasons that my work with young people, and their parents, was effective.

But by the mid-1980s, something was beginning to happen. For reasons too various to go into here in great detail, an invidious line was emerging between where those therapeutic services could be offered, and a subtle split was appearing between those therapeutic services and the role of the social worker in a statutory capacity. Therapeutic and nurturing services were being delivered by voluntary agencies and other caring professionals, and investigations and monitoring were dominating more and more in the work of the statutory child-care worker. This split was perhaps due to greater and greater pressures on more limited resources, external scrutiny and blame as a result of child abuse inquiries, and what workers saw as more and more unrealistic expectations of social workers. I suggest that the insistence in the Children Act and *Working Together* (DHSS, 1978; DoH, 1991i) on strict adherence to procedures and the separation of responsibilities have the effect of institutionalising the kinds of defensive structures that Menzies refers to.

Against a changing political backdrop which redefined the local authority from being a benign purveyor of welfare services to a malevolent bureaucracy intent on taking away personal autonomy and power, this split, resulting in the 'good' services being delegated out of the state sector and the 'bad' services being relegated to the state sector, was becoming inevitable.

Tilman Furniss warns against the splitting of services into care and control agencies in his book, *The Multidisciplinary Handbook of Child Sexual Abuse*. There he warns of the dangers of 'antitherapeutic therapy' (Furniss,1991:93) when the therapist 'keeps secrets' and doesn't use the legal and statutory arena because of a desire to safeguard therapeutic relationships and confidentiality. By not using them, s/he potentially fails to protect the child, or worse still, allows further or worse abuse and psychological damage to occur. He also talks of 'abuse-promoting child protection' (Furniss, 1991:100) which occurs when workers in the protective service act prematurely and without therapeutic insight and which could result in psychological damage which is potentially abusive. This splitting as he sees it, results in damage or danger to the client, and in antagonism between the different workers and agencies involved.

So what does this have to do with partnership? The very structure of a purchasing authority without direct contact with the child or family and the creation of separate services hold within them the potential for projection and splitting. The distance between the client and the worker/agency grows and allows more opportunity for projective defences. This can be manipulated and used by clients, workers and agencies alike to manage their unbearable feelings and anxieties. No worker or agency is allowed to be both good and bad, but rather the possibility of splitting the goodness into one place and the badness into another abounds. This is both anti-therapeutic as well as potentially dysfunctional for the professionals themselves.

Let us look at two possibilities: good purchaser/bad provider or bad purchaser/good provider. If the care manager (purchaser) is seen to be good, any difficulties with the services either in terms of quantity or quality can be attributed to the inadequacy of the provider. The client (and care manager) can then blame the provider for not helping while still maintaining a positive relationship between the care manager and the client. If the purchaser makes decisions about risk and removal, the client has a great deal invested in maintaining this good relationship. On the other hand, if the provider is seen to be good/helpful then all the bad, statutory, powerful, and punitive aspects of working toward change can be located on the care manager/purchaser. Particularly if there is a limited budget and clients do not feel they are getting 'enough', then the bad purchaser is experienced as denying them the necessary help and being withholding.

Both the statutory social worker and the voluntary agency social worker see themselves as genuinely wanting to help. If there is anything that impinges on that helpfulness, there could be a tendency to project the failure (or the anxiety about risk) onto someone or somewhere else. This phenomenon of splitting is made more likely by separating out the place where care is located and the place where control is located into the voluntary and statutory sectors. This inevitably affects the possibility of helpful partnership from a psychodynamic perspective. While it can work well, it also sets up a structure which has the capacity for this type of splitting to occur. This by extension threatens the possibility of true partnership which is about working together; it creates the potential for blame which is anathema to partnership.

So is partnership possible between the statutory, voluntary and/or private sector in child care? The Children Act and *Working Together* say very little about partnership in this arena. Conceptually, partnership is a structural response to a social policy position. In reality it is the manifestation of an ideology of the role of the state in the provision of social services: who pays and who provides. In principle, the idea of partnership between these sectors holds within it the possibility of accountability, creativity and specialism.

Ideally, it is supposed to ensure that the statutory sector and the voluntary sector are made accountable through the use of service level agreements and through detailed costing of services. This, it is suggested, would secure a quality of service and make costing something for which workers could be made 'accountable'. By creativity I mean that, ideally, it allows sectors of service unencumbered by statute to develop a more creative and flexible approach to service delivery. Within the statutory sector, identification of new services would be well documented and could then be negotiated as part of service agreement contracts. This exchange and negotiation process, it is suggested, will ensure a continued development of new and relevant services. By specialism I mean that it is felt that no one agency or section of it can be able to diversify to the extent that it can provide all services to everyone. By encouraging the development of voluntary agencies with specific briefs, it is felt that different agencies will be responsible for different specialisms and thus improve the quality of specialist services.

But is that what we are seeing emerge from the new structures and services? While it is early days, there are indications that these anticipated outcomes are not happening in the ways desired, and some authorities and counties are in fact 'back-pedalling' from their early zealous embrace of the new philosophy. Accountability is laudable if both partners have equal power to define services and service need. If resources (and by that I mean time and personnel as well as direct capital) are not available, then accountability can simply become the redistribution of limited resources with purchasers angry at the limited quality or quantity of purchased service, and providers frustrated by unrealistic service agreement budgets. Tendering for service agreements, while ensuring careful and more realistic budgeting in order to win service contracts, can, however, result in loss of quality through the need to provide less expensive services and in exploitation of one service by the other often in terms of conditions of service for workers.

A belief has developed that one can cost human time and personal interactions. The American model suggests this is possible and social workers are costed at a particular sum per hour calculated on the basis of salary and agency running costs divided by the number of hours they work and their level of productivity measured by number of clients seen. However, many questions still need to be asked. The anticipated creativity has been seen in some instances, but often in terms of 'creative accountancy' where much time is now directed. Top-level workers, supposedly in their positions because of skill in providing services, find themselves in 'business units' struggling with accountancy decisions. The voluntary sector, historically known for its outsider position and ability to set up ' alternative models is now dependent upon service agreements allowing purchasing agencies to define the client group and the nature and type of service. If the purchasing agency needs a particular service it will define the boundaries, and the possibility of 'alternative' or unorthodox services becomes more limited. One would hope that purchaser agencies would purchase more creative services on behalf of its consumers and recognise the needs of minority consumers, but this returns us to the thorny dilemma of purchasers who are not consumers and whose actual customers are the local authority taxpayers. These two ideals of creativity and accountability are sometimes sacrificed as a result of the phenomena of projection and splitting. Thus the potential for success is also inherently the potential for failure of this model.

Finally, the debate about an increase in specialist services was current in social work long before community care legislation redesigned systems and structures. It is not clear how the redistribution of those specialist services between the voluntary and statutory sectors as opposed to within the statutory sector will make those complex issues more clear. The core debate is whether people can be better served by separating their problems into sections to be dealt with by workers with specific skills and knowledge in that area, or by workers who can see the whole person as having a multitude of interrelated difficulties which cannot be easily divided into unconnected parts. The need for workers to hold the needs of the whole person or a whole family within their brief is well documented. The new structure creates purchasers of children's services who are disconnected from purchasers of adult services with competitive budgets. This reduces the potential for working together. Repetition of service or gaps in service are more likely than when there is one overseeing worker. While this model has long disappeared even within the statutory sector, the new structure makes the divide even greater and harder to cross.

I have tried to explore the possibility of voluntary agencies, statutory agencies and the private sector working in partnership in the field of child care and child protection. The complexities of the changes child care professionals work under are great, with implications that extend well beyond our limited remit. We do ourselves and our clients a serious disservice if we do not consider these issues fully and from a number of perspectives. I certainly cannot say that what I have presented is the definitive position. No definitive research has as yet emerged, and transition to different models of child care service provision is being implemented differently and at a different pace across the country. I look forward to a long debate.

Notes

1. Section 59 places voluntary organisations in the same position as local authorities with respect to the provision of accommodation. Section 61 sets out the duties owed in respect of children accommodated by or on behalf of a voluntary organisation. Section 62 sets out the duties of the local authority in relation to any voluntary organisation providing accommodation.
2. Part V – Protection of Children.
3. She now writes under the name of Menzies Lyth.
4. This is an oversimplified and unclinical explanation of projection and splitting. For the purpose of this chapter I hope it will suffice. For a comprehensive understanding of the phenomenon I would recommend the works of Klein, Fenichel, Bion, Heimann and Freud.
5. Masters Degree in Social Work.
6. These are therapeutic phenomena whereby the client transfers feelings and experiences from the past into the present relationship with the worker, and the worker experiences feelings evoked by the relationship with the client. Again, this is an oversimplification of complex psychoanalytic material. For comprehensive clinical definitions I would recommend original source material (Freud, Klein et al.) or the innumerable texts which define and explain these terms for social work and lay consumption.

8   Partnership: a clinical perspective

Mark Berelowitz

The idea that child protection agencies should work in partnership with families seems at first glance to be irresistibly attractive, and also unopposable, rather like Mom and apple pie. After all, who would dare to proclaim that they were against partnership? And of course, I am not opposed to the principle of partnership in child protection. Unfortunately that is not the issue at all. The real issues are first, whether such an idea can work in practice, and, secondly, if it cannot work, what are the dangers of hoping or assuming that it would or should work. I will argue that the whole notion of partnership in child protection is based on mistaken assumptions or pious hopes. These assumptions and hopes have ignored two important issues. The first is to do with the nature of abuse, and the effect that abuse has on those working with children and families. The second is to do with the social structures that impinge upon children's lives. Some indeed have the potential to work in partnership. But others work in a way which is the very antithesis of partnership. I will not attempt here to give a detailed analysis of the many complex effects of abuse, or to discuss in depth the way social services, the health services, the legal system and the press are organised. Rather I will attempt to illustrate key points by means of case examples. I will then go on to argue that the idea of partnership has the potential at best to mislead and disappoint, and at worst to be downright dangerous. My discussion will be from a personal and clinical perspective, as the philosophical, legal and historical issues have been covered elsewhere.

The notion of partnership was introduced to try to counter the natural tendency for social services and the parents to see one another as the enemy as soon as the subject of child abuse rears its head. In one sense it has undoubtedly been helpful because of the message it conveys, from head office as it were, about how people should view one another. It has the useful effect of reminding us that potential adversaries may have some common ground, and that people who have abused their children might still have something important to say about their child's welfare. It also sends a message to solicitors to ensure that their clients co-operate fully with investigative procedures, contact arrangements and the like.

The concept of partnership also made explicit what was already evident in other parts of the child protection fabric, for example the well-established co-operation between various professionals. Judges have received training from child psychiatrists and others about child development, about children's evidence, and about the consequences of child abuse. Indeed it has been gratifying to see how many judges now ensure that Children Act cases are conducted in a way which is respectful to all parties, and with one primary aim of establishing what is best for the child, rather than spending court time on issues of fault and recrimination. This has gone hand in hand with the practice of encouraging expert witnesses to consult with one another before going into the witness box. For example, in a recent case in which I was involved, in which there was a dispute between the estranged parents about the frequency of contact, the judge asked the child psychiatrists to meet together and agree a safe level of contact from the child's point of view, adding that he had no wish to dwell on the rights and wrongs of the case, but simply to find a solution to this particular problem of contact.

All these developments have been very welcome. However, as the major child abuse inquiries of the last ten years have shown, in difficult cases all the prevailing forces seem to militate against the possibility of people working together co-operatively. The major inquiries (Cleveland, Rochdale, Orkney) devour vast sums from the public purse, and lead to recommendations designed to ensure that child abuse 'scandals' should never happen again. However, a key point is unfortunately routinely missed in these inquiries, certainly by the press, and perhaps by government as well. The point is that these celebrated cases which lead to inquiries differ from our day to day work only by degree. All day, every day, throughout the country there are routine child protection cases being dealt with which have at least hints of Cleveland, or Rochdale, or the Orkneys, in terms of how the cases have been processed, and the level of co-operation and suspicion between the parties.

The notion of partnership has, I believe, failed to take into account the personal and public psychological implications of suspicion or allegation of abuse. For the sake of contrast, consider the situation of an offer made to an expectant mother of ante-natal screening tests to discover whether the foetus has any inherited abnormalities or vulnerabilities. Most mothers have these tests and for all practical purposes none require any effort or co-operation from the parents other than allowing a blood sample to be taken or a scan to be performed. Furthermore, none of the tests is compulsory. The test methodology (how the biochemical information is extracted from the blood sample) is opaque to the public, and probably beyond the comprehension of most people. The results of the tests, that is, the risk of abnormality, can be expressed numerically (for example, 1 in a thousand chance of a particular foetal abnormality). Finally, even if the test is abnormal, the doctors still cannot act against the mother's wishes.

In this situation there are of course certain impediments to the development of partnership between mother and obstetrician. But these are as nothing compared to those which confront a social worker and a family trying to achieve partnership where abuse is suspected. Most families are not investigated for child abuse, and do not come under suspicion (despite the fact that child abuse is more common than all foetal abnormalities put together). An enormous amount of co-operation is required if the truth is to be reached. In order to discover the truth an investigation may take place against the wishes of the parents. The 'test methodology' of this investigation is transparent, and everyone, including parents, judges, lawyers and the lay public will have a view about its validity. Any risks and outcomes can be expressed only in crude, imprecise terms (definite, probable, possible, improbable, unlikely, don't know). Finally, if the investigation identifies an 'abnormal finding', action may be taken which overrides the wishes of the parents.

Consider the following case:

Baby Y is brought to hospital by his parents, unconscious. They report that he had been well all day, and then suddenly became unrousable. He had been in their constant care. Physical examination reveals a fractured skull, confirmed on X-ray. The parents say that they have no idea how Baby Y might have hurt his head. Perhaps he was accidentally bumped as he was being put into his cot. Or perhaps his three year old brother Z dropped something on him. Baby Y dies. The pathologist reports that his head injury is consistent with being held by the heels and swung, so that his head smashed against a solid flat surface. There is also a fractured rib and bruising of the internal organs.

A social worker and policeman visit the home, and find, on the wall near the baby's cot, a head-sized dent, with a few blood flecks around it, and a few baby hairs. The pathologist's explanation gains plausibility, and the parents are charged with murder. Each says 'I didn't do it, and he (she) couldn't have done it.' The trial judge instructs the jury to find both parents not guilty, as no mechanism exists for deciding who delivered the fatal blow.

A social worker is now expected to work in partnership with this family in planning the future care of brother Z. But what on earth does partnership mean here? The parents say that Z is difficult, and tells lots of fibs. Should this be believed and taken into account when finding foster parents. The mother says that she loves Z, and wants lots of contact. Should this be permitted if she maintains her view about the death of Y? Does it make a difference if the parents are poor, or if they are amphetamine addicts, or if the mother was sexually abused, or if the father was brutally beaten as a child?

I am sure that it is beyond the capacity of most social workers (or anyone else) to have a partnership in anything like the ordinary sense with a family like this. The one partnership which has persisted in the family, that between the parents, has supported and concealed gross cruelty and deception. Who would offer (or dare) to enter into a straight and honest relationship with these parents? And how will the partnership survive the discovery that the mother is pregnant again?

Consider Ronald, aged 10, who told his aunt that his father had sodomised him. He repeated this story to the police, but retracted it when the tape recorder was turned on. He and his 14 year old sister Dana were removed from home and placed in separate children's homes. The sister made allusive comments about sexual and physical abuse to the children's home staff. There was a suggestion that her mother had prostituted her once, when she was ten, when father was in prison and they were short of money. The parents denied any abuse. At one interview the father made it plain to the social worker that he knew her home address, and the ages and appearance of her children. The mother was noted to have black eyes, regularly. She said that these were always caused by banging into things accidentally.

When the parents and children were seen by a child psychiatrist, they all stood up and began screaming in unison at the psychiatrist insisting that they were a normal family, and that everyone should leave them alone and let them live together again.

The specialist child protection social workers and the staff at Dana's children's home thought that both children had been abused by father and others, and presented their case to the court. Ronald's residential care workers took a different view, namely that this was an ordinary family who had been abused by social services. They helped Ronald type long and detailed letters to the High Court, extolling the virtues of his father. They also encouraged the father to make a complaint against the psychiatrist, encouraging him in his view that because the psychiatrist had not permitted father and children to smoke during the interview, the psychiatrist had therefore provoked the father into calling him a 'fucking arsehole' and threatening to knock his head off. The policeman raised his voice to Ronald when Ronald, on videotape, retracted all his allegations. Most importantly, Ronald's residential social workers simply stopped talking to their colleagues in the child protection team, and refused to obey direct instructions from their senior management.

Now this was clearly a case in which it was unlikely that the full truth would ever be known. But any chance of this inconclusive outcome being admitted was excluded completely by the two opposing views, the one stating that abuse had taken place, the other, that it had not. No partnership of any reasonable kind existed. Everyone viewed everyone else as being in unholy alliances, and no-one had a sense of working together. The judge said that the family life was most unsatisfactory, and the father extraordinarily unpleasant, but that the evidence did not permit him to make a finding of child sexual abuse. The father's barrister later confided privately to the child psychiatrist that his client had sexually abused the children. Of that she had no doubt. But the Local Authority case had been destroyed by their own internal wrangling.

This was in many ways a simple case. Children's lives were not at risk. The hard evidence was limited in the extreme. The children were articulate, and there were no drawings or dreams to interpret. Different hypotheses might explain the facts, but no hypothesis was compelling. And yet the case managed to get under everyone's skin to such an extent that partnership did not exist at all. In fact, one can see in this little case many of the elements of Cleveland or the Orkneys, in terms of how people failed to work together.

In these two cases we can identify some of the impediments to partnership. In both cases, but especially the second, the parents did not agree to work in partnership. In fact, in the second case, the entire family decided that the social agencies were acting against the best interests of the family. Clearly one cannot enter into a partnership with a partner who is wholly unwilling; one is reminded here of shotgun weddings. Furthermore, the Children Act does not make it clear who the primary partners should be. Should the partnership be with the parents, or the family, or the teenage child? How does one manage the partnership when the various partners are in direct conflict with one another? The obvious conflict in both the above examples is of course that between the parents and social services. In the Case of Z above, it soon became clear that Z was not, and did not wish to be in any sort of partnership with his mother. Although he did not use these exact words, he made plain his feeling that his welfare was being undermined by the efforts to accommodate his mother's wishes.

In the case of Ronald, there was a different sort of partnership problem, in which Social Services split into two competing partners. Could the mother, or the guardian ad litem, or the child be in partnership with both these parties? Clearly not. Finally, one should not forget the partnership between professionals, which might be seen as far more important than that between agency and child. The child psychiatrist invited Ronald's legal team to subpoena the father's barrister, so that her comment about father's guilt might be repeated in Court. But this request was rejected on the grounds that it was likely to 'cause problems.'

It is not my intention here to provide a full explanation of why child abuse has this effect on the behaviour of trained professionals, and why partnership becomes impossible. But one can note certain points. Children are the focus of much emotion, abused children especially so. There is no room in these cases for difference of opinion, as there is in so many other areas. Two doctors might disagree about whether a patient has hepatitis or glandular fever.

They are free, with the consent of the patient, to agree to disagree, and to treat the patient for one condition only, on a trial basis. If proven wrong, the treatment will be changed. But no such luxury exists in child abuse cases. Someone who is convinced that a child has been abused, or is at risk, cannot agree to disagree with someone holding a conflicting opinion. Instead, the professionals sometimes 'play dirty'.

These cases do not, to put it mildly, lend themselves to partnership. Instead, the forces align to prevent it.

Partnership is put under special strain when child sexual abuse is alleged in the context of divorce proceedings. I have yet to come across a case in which the views of the accused parent in the dispute have been sought by social services. This type of case is indeed the best test of the viability of the partnership concept, as it requires the social workers to be the partners of people with apparently sharply divergent views. It will be virtually impossible for social workers (or any one else) to remember both accounts, and still to work in partnership with both parents. They might just manage, provided they didn't have to be responsible for the child's welfare as well. This makes the task impossible. Invariably, one parent is rejected as a partner by the local authority. This can always be justified post hoc, but it has led to a number of incorrect child care decisions, and always makes the court proceedings much more acrimonious than they might have been.

Unfortunately the psychological complexity of these cases is not the only impediment to partnership. There are other impediments as well, some of them structural. Imagine a football game in which the first half is played by one set of rules, and then a new set of rules is introduced in the second half, with retrospective effect over the first half too. Handling of the ball is permitted in the first half, but outlawed in the second, so that at the start of the second the referee penalises everyone who handled in the first. Who would agree to play a game like this? Yet this is exactly what happens in child abuse cases. Let me try to explain.

When a case first comes to light, the investigating services uphold the principles of both partnership, and paramountcy of the child's welfare. But when it comes to court, it is an entirely different matter. Legal counsel do not have to act in partnership, and are free from the obligation to give paramountcy to the child's welfare. And if something goes wrong, and the newspapers lay into the social workers, no principles of partnership apply at all. Under the tabloid rules of the game, applied post hoc to earlier actions undertaken in the spirit of partnership, anything can be made to look reckless and stupid.

Take for example the mother of brothers Y and Z. Y dies, and Z is adopted. The mother leaves her partner, after telling social workers that he killed Y and beat Z. She forms a new relationship, and seems to live a reasonable life. Five years on, she becomes pregnant.

A case conference decides to allow her a fresh start, and to work with her in looking after the new baby B. This may or may not be the right decision. But if baby B is killed, it will be quite impossible to argue subsequently that the right decision at the time of B's birth was to allow his mother to care for him. Even if, on all the evidence available at that time, it had appeared to be the right decision, it would be impossible to argue this later. Except perhaps to the most sophisticated members of the press and public, the belief that the right decision was made initially will simply not be acceptable. Certainly, it would not stop the popular newspapers from vilifying the social workers.

Not surprisingly, many social workers and others in child protection feel that everyone is their enemy, and that they must always be on their guard. Any social worker or health visitor who reads the newspapers will know that a career can be destroyed by a mistake on a child protection case. This leads to defensiveness of many different kinds. It certainly does not lead to an atmosphere where people might say to one another 'That's a really interesting idea. We hadn't thought of that ourselves.'

Look at the effect that this has on social workers in the field.

'Hello, is that the duty desk.'
'Yes.'
'This is doctor X from Hospital Y. To whom am I speaking please?'
'A social worker.'
'I wish to report a child abuse matter to you. Can you tell me your name please.'
'We don't give out our names.'
'You can't really expect me to discuss a serious matter like this without knowing who I am talking to.'
Silence.
'Look, I won't tell you the child's name, unless you tell me your name and title please.'
Silence.
'Could I please speak to the duty senior.'

Or consider the case of the clinic which tried repeatedly over nine months to persuade Social Services to have a child protection case conference about a particular child. Eventually they agreed. The Social Services clerk rang to inform the referrer of the date and time of the conference. The referrer was going to be out of the country on that particular day. 'Well', said the clerk, 'That's the time, and we can't change it now.' The referrer replied that it was he who raised the alarm about the case, and only he had any direct knowledge of the family and the children. 'That's tough', said the clerk. 'We're not changing the time just for you'. The referrer spoke to the duty senior, who also refused to change the time. It later became clear why. That particular area office was about to be closed, and, from an organisational point of view, was hanging by a thread. It was a considerable achievement for them to arrange a conference at all. To expect them then to re-arrange it was simply unthinkable.

The legal profession plays its part too in ensuring that partnership doesn't work. Everyone involved in child care cases, including all the parties, is required to work in partnership to give paramountcy to the child's welfare; that is, everyone except the solicitors and barristers. To return to my sporting analogy above, consider a game in which most of the team play by one set of rules, but the conduct of certain key players is governed by a wholly different set of rules.

Take for example Anna, age 4, whose parents were divorced, and whose stepfather sexually abused her. It was agreed by all parties that she could not stay with her mother. The guardian wanted Anna to go to her father and his new wife. The local authority were opposed to this, because they did not feel that the father had the right attitude to sexual abuse. The judge was inexperienced in this area. Also, he was ill, and was inclined therefore to pay more attention to headlines and bullet points than to detail. Nobody knew this better than the local authority barrister, who questioned the father's new wife thus, according to the notes taken in court:

> **Barrister:** 'Lets say Anna does come to live with you. What would you do if Anna asks you if she can tell her school friends about the sexual abuse?'
> **Wife:** 'I would explain that it was private, and that she should discuss it only with dad and me for now.'
> **Barrister:** 'Private? What do you mean?'
> **Wife:** 'Well, you know, like it's personal. Also it wouldn't help her to have her school friends know about it.'
> **Barrister:** 'What do you mean, personal?'
> **Wife:** 'I dunno ... like secret, I suppose. I mean you don't want to tell everyone about it.'
> **Barrister:** (exploding with feigned anger, as she finally gets the key word for which she had been fishing): 'Secret! Do you mean to tell me that you would tell a sexually abused girl to keep secrets? Don't you read the newspapers? Don't you know that that's what abusers say? That's how girls get abused. Secrets! It's quite unbelievable. Forgive me, Your Lordship, but I just cannot believe that a woman would say a thing like that in this day and age. Isn't it a disgrace! Secrets! To a sexually abused child. Surely you cannot believe that you are fit to be a mother, with ideas like that!'

During the break, several people remonstrated with the barrister. It was clear that she had been fishing for the word 'secret', knowing the effect that this would have on the judge. She said that she was acting on instructions. The local authority was asked if this were true. Well, yes and no, was the reply. They didn't want the child to go to the father and his wife. Also they didn't approve of the line of questioning, and agreed that it was deliberately misleading. However, the barrister had sole responsibility for the conduct of the case, and they would not interfere with her in any way. Certainly they would continue to use her services. After all, she helped them win cases.

I hope that this (true) example shows just how partnership collapses under the pressure of the courtroom atmosphere, how the legal process interposes itself between those who are supposed to be working together in co-operation.

Barristers can undermine partnership in more subtle ways too. In the custody and contact case described above, the judge asked the two psychiatrists to meet with each of the parents separately, without counsel, to conduct as it were a clinical interview with them, in which the children's needs would be fully discussed. Perhaps then a compromise might be reached between the warring parents, and a contested hearing avoided. And indeed this was achieved. The two psychiatrists spent half an hour with each parent, and obtained a satisfactory compromise to which all parties agreed. They reported this back to the judge. 'Hang on a moment.' said counsel. 'I need to confer with my client.' Five minutes later, the offer of compromise was withdrawn, and the contested hearing proceeded.

Of course not all barristers do this. Some clearly do their best to persuade clients to change their instructions where these instructions are counterproductive. But it is not a question only of substance, but also of style. I would argue that it is within the spirit of partnership to force an expert witness to think critically about his or her own ideas. Indeed any competent expert welcomes this. Yet we all know many barristers who seek deliberately to confuse or muddle witnesses, to make them seem stupid, while avoiding critical analysis of the witnesses' argument itself. Clearly there are degrees of partnership, and one can take a hard or soft approach.

There is one last problem with partnership, perhaps the most important of all. The very word does not lend itself to precise definition, and certainly it cannot be operationalised. To most of us it probably means the following: respect for the views of others; treating people like human beings; and not adopting a fixed attitude. But to many workers in the field it has clearly meant something else, namely bending over backwards to please, or even entering into a kind of competition to see who can be the greatest friend to the child and family, as in the case of Ronald. I am sure that this was not the intention of the legislators, but anyone who knows anything about social work training, and about the pressure on social workers in the field, would have anticipated this.

In my clinical practice, I have not observed partnership to work successfully. Partnership implies consent, honesty, respect, equality and freedom to disagree. It also requires tolerance of mistakes, and the capacity to forgive honest errors. I hope that I have shown that these qualities are unlikely to be present in most child abuse cases. And even if they were to be substantially present in the handling of a case, when it gets to court, the gloves will come off. And when it gets to the tabloids, the knives will be out. There will be little respect, no freedom to disagree, and no forgiving of mistakes.

It is not clear to me what the overall solution might be. There are some pointers. All professionals in the field need to be steeped in critical analysis of their own ideas and practices. In particular they need to learn that they don't know everything. Field workers need to be looked after very well by their managers, and the managers by the policy-makers. A local authority that cannot afford to employ typists and minute takers cannot run an effective child protection service.

Judges can strive to create a suitable atmosphere in court, where destructive questioning is not tolerated, and where witnesses are respected for changing their minds, or indicating that they have no answer to a particular question.

Journalists might approach the subject in a more measured way, looking more critically at the limits to effective action in a particular case. Equally the media might do more to encourage good parenting, rather than focusing on the failure to detect bad parenting.

What is really needed of course is a national effort to encourage a real partnership within society on behalf of children and those who care for or work with them. This is not a partnership about child protection, but rather a partnership in promoting child health, welfare and education. Until we make very much more progress in this area, partnership in child protection will be at best a dream, and we will forever be shutting the stable door as the horse bolts past us.

Part D: Constructing partnership

9 Child protection and working in partnership with parents

Sarah Woodhouse

Introduction

The intersection of child protection and partnership has raised sharp questions about the philosophy and practice of partnership for social work practitioners and for policy-makers alike. This chapter reflects upon the practice observed during fieldwork in three social services departments during 1992-3 in the context of the assumptions underlying the child protection system.

The Children Act makes the broad scope of the concept clear: partnership with parents is intended to be a guiding model for the relationship between parents and social workers in most cases of social services involvement. However, while my research found that there is support and enthusiasm for the philosophy of partnership amongst social workers it also revealed that many social workers express uncertainty and hesitancy about how to put the theory into practice, and, specifically, whether it can and should be applied to child protection cases. This chapter will examine briefly some of the background to the Children Act and in particular the employment of partnership as a legitimising ideology for social services involvement with children, and sheds some light on the current ambiguities and tensions being expressed by social workers. The theme that runs throughout this article is that the Children Act itself leaves many central pre-existing tensions in social work unresolved and, as a result, practitioners still find themselves negotiating a balance between conflicting ideas and interests in their practice.

Specifically, this chapter will question the appropriateness of an undifferentiated vision of partnership as an informing concept for practice in a wide variety of casework situations and will address the difficulties raised by the dominant model, evident in the official documentation about the Act, of the social worker/parent relationship. It will suggest, as does Judith Masson (pp.27-33), that a differentiated model of the relationship can help us develop a clearer vision of the application of partnership to child protection cases.

Partnership and legitimation of social work interventions

The Children Act was passed at a time when there were misgivings about the effectiveness of social work in terms of either protecting children (through effecting changes in the behaviour of parents or recognising when there was a need to remove children at risk) or respecting the rights of parents/families. The Act is characterised by the attempt to (re)construct a consensus about intervention through balancing competing interests: it has, for example, been portrayed as an 'uneasy synthesis' of different value perspectives, most prominent being those of state paternalism and the defence of the birth family. This results in an attempt to better protect both the child and the parent, and therefore in 'bidirectional policy' (Fox-Harding, 1991). The current preoccupation with partnership represents in part, therefore, a concern to legitimise social work interventions at a time when the various controversies around child protection cases have added fuel to a more general concern about the role of the state versus the individual. Not surprisingly, partnership as a concept is designed to meet the difficult policy dilemmas that interventions into families pose in a political climate that values simultaneously the protection of children, the primacy of the birth family and the rights of both parents and children.

What is it about partnership that unites these conflicting interests? How is it that partnership can satisfy these different value perspectives? The language of partnership is important, because terms such as consent, agreement, cooperation, involvement, participation and voluntary partnership draw us into a vision which suggests that even child protection work can be free of conflict and coercion. This is a highly appealing picture of the future of social work for practitioners and policy makers alike.[1] Partnership may also operate as a powerful legitimiser of state (social work) interventions. In a case where there are concerns about protecting the child and the parent accepts intervention (perhaps to accommodate the child), it is the consent of the parent which authorises that intervention. In this case voluntary partnership meets the demands of parental rights while simultaneously offering protection for the child.

The Department of Health Guidance and Regulations (1991e) emphasize the need for a partnership between the local authority and parents to ensure that children are returned to their families in a planned way.[2] In addition they indicate that the removal of some of the legal resources that local authorities formerly had available to them has been accompanied by a reliance on the willingness of social workers and parents to co-operate in a partnership and reach agreements which will achieve in practical terms precisely the same outcomes for the family as were obtained through the deployment of the former legal powers.

Alternatively, where there is a child protection concern, social services can use the legal process to ask the court to make an order which sets in motion the rules and legal procedures for judicial decision-making with their protections of the rights of parents under the Children Act (for example, the presumption of no order). These procedural and substantive protections are additionally supported by the expectation that social services will continue to work in partnership with the parent in a similar way to the parallel case of accommodation under a voluntary partnership where no order has been obtained.

The provisions of the Act are backed up by a series of regulations which specify in some detail practical measures to ensure the increased involvement of parents and their increased control. These apply whether or not there is a court order in force. For example it is required:

- That local authorities engage in detailed planning for the child; parents would normally be involved and kept informed of significant changes and developments in that plan which would include placement decisions (Arrangements for the Placement of Children Regulations);

- That local authorities regularly review cases of children provided with accommodation which should involve ascertaining the wishes and feelings of parents (Review of Children's Cases Regulations);

- That written agreements be drawn up where children are accommodated, to specify in some detail the respective responsibilities of child, parent and local authority: parental responsibility remains with the parent except in so far as it is delegated to the local authority in the written agreement or passed to the local authority by a court order;[3] and

- That local authorities, voluntary organisations and registered children's homes establish a procedure for considering representations, including complaints, about children's services.[4]

In summary, so far as the relationship of social workers with parents is concerned, the Children Act envisages two types of partnership: the voluntary partnership which deals with situations where there is no court order in relation to the child and legal control remains in the hands of the parent, and the non-voluntary partnership where a court has made an order and varying degrees of control pass to the local authority. However, even in the case of a Care Order giving the local authority parental responsibility for the child, attempts to consult with and involve parents must still be made.

The empirical research

The main body of this research involved a detailed, in-depth study of the implementation and practice of partnership in one local authority. It concentrated on social workers' perceptions of partnership, and did not cover the perceptions of parents, children and other professionals. Interviews with senior management and middle management were complemented by following sixteen cases through interviews with the social workers, and attendance as an observer at case conferences and review and planning meetings. Although the actual circumstances varied considerably, most of the cases in the sample involved children under the age of eleven about whom social workers had child protection concerns. With the exception of a case involving respite care for a disabled child, these were cases where, in the assessment of the social worker, there were grounds for a court order but where a voluntary approach had been chosen instead of a compulsory route.

This study was followed up in another local authority through interviews with senior and middle management, and in a third by interviews with senior managers.

Modelling the parent/social worker relationship

The Children Act and the concept of partnership are based on a particular model of parent and social worker, and the way they relate to each other. Models are constructs that allow us to make sense of the world. They are systems of meaning that extract elements from our surroundings as significant and arrange them in relation to each other, insist on similarities and points of departure, and provide a lens through which we can begin to view the world. The vision they produce is thus a refracted one. I will argue that the model of the parent/social worker relationship does not encompass the totality of the experience of social workers. Secondly I will suggest that partnership has been most developed and tested by successful respite care schemes, and that this in itself indicates that the assumptions about the casework relationship underlying the partnership principle have serious limitations. Thirdly I will draw attention to the wide range of situations where partnership is envisaged as operating and argue from this that a more differentiated model is required.

The dominant model of the casework relationship in voluntary partnership is a consensus model. Put crudely this can be caricatured as assuming four key elements:

● The rational parent.

● The social worker with infinite time and patience.

● The sharing of control and power.

● A coincident understanding shared by parent and social worker (of what the problems are and what the solutions to them might be).

In this model the 'good' social worker and the 'good' parent are defined by their ability to agree on what constitutes the child's best interests.

The rational parent

Firstly the model assumes that parents will behave in a rational manner and that this will necessarily mean that they will understand their child's best interests in the same way as a social worker or legislator might. For example the Guidance and Regulations state 'Parents who are seeking to agree arrangements in their child's best interests will appreciate the need to minimise disruption to the child' (DoH, 1991g:para.3.28).

This very clearly illustrates the sort of assumptions about the rational parent on which voluntary partnership is based. Such a parent will put the child's interests first even in what may be emotionally charged situations and will appreciate, for example, the sort of trauma a return home may involve for a child who has been accommodated away from home for some time. The social workers interviewed did not, however, view parents in this way, and expressed concerns that parents might suddenly withdraw their child(ren) from accommodation under a voluntary agreement.

The assumption that parents are rational is not consistently maintained. For example, no. 6 of the 'Principles of Good Child Care Practice' states that:

Parents are individuals with needs of their own. Even though services may be offered primarily on behalf of their children, parents are entitled to help and consideration in their own right. Just as some young people are more vulnerable than others, so are some mothers and fathers. Their parenting capacity may be limited temporarily or permanently by poverty, racism, poor housing or unemployment or by personal or marital problems, sensory or physical disability, mental illness or past life experiences. Lack of parenting skills or inability to provide adequate care should not be equated with lack of affection or with irresponsibility (DoH, 1989a).

The child welfare system expects that parents will act responsibly, but at the same time clearly recognises that parents have interests of their own and may be struggling with a whole range of problems, the implication being that parents will not always act with their child's best interests in mind. These conflicting expectations about the behaviour of parents are most likely to be apparent where 'parenting capacity' is limited by one of the factors set out above and, therefore, the family is subject to child protection concerns. Social workers found it especially difficult to set up a partnership with such parents, facing difficulties in building trust and understanding and finding strategies to eliminate inherent imbalances of power.

The social worker with infinite time and patience

Lack of resources in many social services departments may well be an important factor contributing to difficulties in working in partnership. It has been well documented, particularly by the child death inquiries of the 1980s, that social services departments are frequently overstretched and, as a result, social workers might be operating under great pressure.

Social workers when interviewed emphasised that partnership is time consuming and demands a higher level of resources than other methods of working. Overstretched social workers and departmental resources are therefore a great inhibitor in the development of this style of working and yet the consensus model assumes a social worker with infinite time, resources and patience.

Sharing of control and power

Partnership requires a realignment of the casework relationship, to one where control and power are shared. As we have seen, some of the regulations are designed to encourage this, for example requiring social workers to involve parents in decision-making. However, social workers have a large amount of discretion about the rigour with which these regulations are applied. As one social worker admitted, 'written agreements are sometimes not really agreements at all'. One case that illustrates this concerned a mother whose parenting capacities were seen as limited, but although social services had tried several different strategies to help her to develop skills, her behaviour appeared to have altered little. She continued to be co-operative in matters such as allowing access and asking for respite care but her ability and/or willingness to change were both in question. The social worker had drawn up a written agreement, which the mother had signed, and this was seen as her last chance. When there was a further failure to meet some fairly specific goals then the agreement itself would be evidence that could be used in court that partnership had been tried and had failed and that grounds for making an order existed. In other cases too it was thought probable (or even inevitable) that parents would be unable to deliver the goods, and in such cases the primary function of the agreement was described as potential evidence that partnership had been tried and has failed.

This illustrates that the form partnership takes can be influenced by the proximity of a decision to apply for a care order. Social workers' attention can be focused in two directions at once when attempting to work in voluntary partnership while preparing evidence for compulsory intervention.

Another important value in partnership is openness and honesty between social workers and clients but openness can have coercive aspects when what is being shared with parents is a plan to apply for a court order if, for example, the parent does not agree to allow the local authority to accommodate the child. This is something akin to 'bargaining in the shadow of the law' where grounds for a care order exist in the perception of the local authority. Even if social workers are making inaccurate assumptions about legal powers available to them, it is their definitions that count: few clients have sufficient knowledge of the content of legal powers or access to professional advice to propose alternatives and to negotiate authoritatively. Disparities in knowledge and experience between social workers and parents need to be addressed in definitions of what is meant by partnership. As Kaganas has pointed out (p.13), social workers can be seen as repeat players, who have the opportunity to become experienced in how the system works, and to a certain extent shape it to their requirements through selective use of legal resources such as the courts and privileged access to legal advice.[5]

Coincident understanding shared by parent and social worker

It is also assumed that parents and social workers share a vision about what the problems are and what the response should be. This was not always the situation in the cases that I followed. In some, parents were seen as not taking the concerns of social services seriously enough, while in others parents were pushing for the child to be returned home while social workers were resisting. Social workers may not always realise that there are divergent perceptions: they may believe that a consensus has emerged and that the relationship is functioning as a partnership, precisely because the way that the parents experience the relationship is invisible to them.

Respite care, and the need for a reformulated model

Respite care and the development of partnership

There has been little research which indicates in positive terms how a partnership between parents and social workers might be established, or the circumstances in which it is most viable. Research completed before the implementation of the Act indicates that compulsory measures are often counter-productive in terms of maintaining family ties and preserving a good relationship between parents and social workers (DoH, 1991g). The 'most encouraging indications for partnership' (DoH, 1991g) which are mentioned come from the studies which have been done on the success of respite care, dealing mostly with short-term relief given to families by the care of children with disabilities, for example Aldgate and Webb's Oxfordshire research. Although some of the problems are touched upon, these are not developed, and remain submerged in the generally favourable prognosis for partnership that these studies are used to support.

Respite care is probably an ideal situation as far as carrying through partnership into the casework relationship is concerned. It exemplifies the type of circumstances where the model of the consumer family using the services of local authorities is most appropriate. There is likely to be a degree of consensus between the social worker and parent about what the problems are and what are the most appropriate measures to deal with them. This consensus makes it more likely that the demands of the parent will be seen as rational, that is, coinciding with the definitions of the professionals as to the best interests of the child, and also that the actions of social workers will match definitions of good practice since they will be legitimated by agreement. The short term break from the stresses of caring for a child with disabilities is by definition what respite care is all about, and it is a good candidate for partnership since there is less scope for the emergence of conflict. It is easier to share power and control in such situations too, where there are not child protection concerns.

Child protection concerns

One major concern raised by partnership is that it potentially encourages confusion about who the client is, and the view of the child as client gets lost in building a relationship with the parent. *A Child In Trust* (London Borough of Brent, 1985) emphasised that the child is the client not the parent, and it is the child's interests that should take priority where child protection work is being done. Such statements are largely a response to the dilemma of professionals who work with families where it is possible to see both parents and children as potential clients and feel the pull of each, which can be manifested in a tendency, identified by *A Child in Trust*, to use children as instrumental to the treatment of their parents' problems.

This tendency is reproduced to some extent in the Children Act: in 'Principles and Practice in Regulations and Guidance' (DoH, 1989a) a certain ambiguity is expressed in a list of principles of good child care practice. Some of these principles assert the priority of the child's welfare and others the legitimacy of the interests of parents as individuals in their own right, with needs of their own, entitled to help and consideration. It is not made clear in any detail how exactly these two elements of good practice should mesh together, and it is likely that in the majority of cases social workers negotiate the issue on the ground on a case-by-case basis. During the research, social workers drew attention to the complexity of interaction between these principles. In particular the best interests of a child were often seen to involve an element of meeting the needs and concerns of parents. For example in one case an ageing parent was being assisted in coming to terms with his incapacity to care for his two daughters, whose welfare was endangered by the standard of care he was capable of providing. As an alternative home was sought, assisting him to accept the situation and involving him in finding suitable carers undoubtably slowed the process, but his support of the new carers as a result of the time and care invested was essential to his daughters' acceptance of them. In another case the social worker prioritised the need to address the father's alcoholism and the relationship between the parents in order to find a way to return a child home. These are examples of thoughtful practice, but they do show the potential difficulty of balancing considerations that are interrelated, and which partly rely for their success on predicting future behaviour.

So, despite the universal support expressed by social workers for the philosophy of voluntary partnership, there were recurring apprehensions. Fears were voiced that potentially a conflict could emerge between the best interests of the child and partnership with parents, and that some children would not be properly protected as a result. These interests at times coalesce but can also diverge, and social workers found it difficult to judge when they diverge, particularly when making predictions about the future behaviour of parents. This is an issue that has not been resolved clearly on a policy level and social workers seemed to be left with a sense that a worrying question-mark hung over some of their casework.

Part Three of the Children Act is subtitled *Provision of services for children and their families*. Where there is no court order, the local authority is essentially acting as a provider of these services, which include respite care, accommodation and family aides. The question of who is the recipient of services is not a crucial one where there is no child protection issue involved. However, service provision is also seen as an appropriate response in child protection cases and here the dilemma about how to remain clear about who is the client is reflected in the way that 'family', 'child' and 'parent' were used interchangeably by social workers. This is also a feature of some of the literature.[6]

The Guidance and Regulations (DoH, 1991e) state that, where grounds for a compulsory order exist, 'in the majority of cases local authorities will be able to agree on an arrangement that will best provide for the needs of the child and safeguard and promote his welfare'. Interviews with local authority solicitors and social workers revealed that the decision to institute court proceedings was usually prompted by the severity of abuse combined with unco-operative parents, and that the latter was the key factor.

There were different perceptions about the attitudes of the courts to making orders in different areas, and in one local authority social workers and their managers said that the court process was 'stacked against the local authority'. This was attributed to a misinterpretation by judges and magistrates of the Act, especially its 'presumption of no order' and its emphasis on partnership which led to court orders being seen by courts as necessarily bad. In the view of workers in the local authority such misinterpretation of the Act meant that vulnerable children could be left unprotected. Personnel in all three local authorities commented that courts are reluctant to make orders where partnership has not been attempted.

The need for a reformulated model

As we move further away from the respite care situation and the vision of the family as consumer of local authority services, and through child protection cases to a relationship firmly underpinned by the possibility or actuality of compulsion, doubts about the rationality of the parent become stronger, there is more need for time and resources, social workers are more anxious about a lack of control and power, and conflicting understandings are more likely. An alternative model is needed which acknowledges the problems inherent in a partnership between parties with very different access to resources and takes a more realistic view of the sort of difficulties facing many of the clients of social services departments as well as those facing social workers. This would allow for a more fruitful discussion of how such difficulties might be overcome.

Conclusion

Almost all social workers I talked to identified partnership with parents as a very significant part of the Children Act or even as the most important of its innovations. However, it also emerged that there is confusion in thinking about the circumstances in which partnership is possible and about what it might mean in terms of practical social work. This is a reflection of the embryonic stage of the thinking that has been done about these issues by researchers, academics, and policy makers.

Voluntarism and consent are a language of legitimation around which a political and practice consensus can be built. However it is in the practicalities of implementation that doubts and questions have emerged at points of conflict between different value perspectives and the relative priorities given to them. Social workers are resolving many issues in their case work, and there is a need for more fine tuning of the practice of partnership in order for it to be more effective in involving parents and protecting children simultaneously.

Notes

1. Whether partnership in practice lives up to these expectations is the subject matter of the second half of this article. However, there are suggestions that conflicts remain at the level of policy. Fox Harding (1991b) remains unclear whether a satisfactory and workable balance between competing value perspectives can be found and if so whether the Children Act represents this. Parton (1991:192) states that many found the resulting compromises 'difficult to support'.
2. The Children Act removed the power of local authorities to pass a Parental Rights Resolution or to require 28 days' notice before removing a child from voluntary care. These two changes to the formal legal powers of local authorities are reinforced by a significant change of terminology, so that 'voluntary care' has disappeared and we now talk of the 'accommodation' of children, who are no longer in the 'care' of the local authority but are 'looked after' by them.
3. Schedule 4 Reg 4(2).
4. Section 26(3)-(8); s59(4); para. 10(2)(1) of Schedule 6 and para. 6 of Schedule 7.
5. In addition, even where social workers perceive that the relationship reflects the values of partnership, they may be mistaken. The 'DATA syndrome' (Marsh quoted in Department of Health, 1991g) has been used to characterise the response of social workers claiming that they are 'Doing All This Already' when they are not. The DATA syndrome points to the gap between the perceptions social workers have of what they are doing and what it is that they are actually doing. There may be a tendency to see co-operation developing even when it is not.
6. Parton (1991:155) uses first the term 'family' and then 'parents' to describe the recipients of services provided by the local authority.

10 Partnership in politics and law: a new deal for parents?

Michael King

1.

For anyone involved in tracing the recent evolution of the knowledge and practices that society has selected and employed to deal with the difficult problem of how to assure its own reproduction through the medium of the family, the dominant part played by law must be something of a surprise. It is certainly true that in the past law, in the form of rights of succession and inheritance regulating the legitimacy of claims to title and property, played an important role. But this was largely that of persuading parents of the importance of exercising control over their children's choice of marital partner in ways that were likely to maximize the chances of continuity and the smooth transition of money, power and property from one generation to the next.[1] This control took a particularly virulent form in education, particularly of women, who were systematically excluded from seats of learning and from liberal professions and trained in those skills that were likely to make them attractive to the most eligible male suitors. Today, society's continuity is seen as depending much more upon the acquisition by both sexes of educational and professional qualifications, skills and technical expertise, and ultimately upon the 'correct' combination of nature and nurture predisposing the fortunate child to such acquisitions. It is perhaps surprising, therefore, to find the legal system, rather than child welfare, science, education, health, or economics still playing the part of overseer in relation to the upbringing of children.

Given the pervasive success of science and medicine in formulating and offering solutions to so many of society's problems from the mid-eighteenth century, one would perhaps have expected the combination of these two social systems to have dominated totally society's understanding of what children needed to allow them to develop into socially adapted adults and the processes by which such needs might be met. Indeed, it seemed for a period in the latter part of the nineteenth and the first half of the twentieth century that the social construction of children and childhood would develop along these lines. Social evolutionism, eugenics, hygienics and later

I should like to thank Patrick Parkinson and Alison Diduck for their useful comments on earlier versions of this chapter.

psychoanalysis, paediatrics and developmental psychology all laid claim to the securing of a better future for children and for society. It appeared for a time that a social consensus would be bound to emerge over issues of right or wrong for children and that this consensus would depend upon universal notions of health and psychological well-being legitimated by science. These optimistic predictions, however, reckoned without paying sufficient attention to the disruptive effects of politically generated conflicts and, to a lesser extent, of disputes within philosophy over what constitutes 'the good life' and within economics, as to how that good life can be achieved.

To the sociological observer, the failure of predictions and the disappointment of expectations generated within one socially functional system, such as health or science are, of course, to be expected, since there is no way for that system to know in advance the ways in which other social systems, such as law and politics, are likely to reconstruct and respond to its communications (Luhmann, 1977; Luhmann, 1992b).

Even the best sociologists themselves are at a loss when it comes to predicting with any precision what kind of disruptions are likely to occur to the social order and anticipating the precise events which will cause significant anxieties for society and lead eventually to new and more acceptable social formulations of problems and the way to solve them (Luhmann, 1976; Luhmann, 1986a; Luhmann, 1986b; Luhmann, 1988; Luhmann, 1990b).

2.

It is not the purpose of this chapter to attempt the impossible by providing a step-by-step objective, historical account of the causes of law's present popularity in the production of socially acceptable versions of what is required of families in their contribution to the reproduction of a safe and stable society. On the other hand, it is both intellectually legitimate and theoretically possible to identify those factors which appear to have led to the lack of confidence in the kind of universal truths and politically neutral versions offered by the scientific and medical accounts.

Put in general terms, much of what passes for social analysis today is founded upon ideological models which emphasise gender, class, and ethnic (including culture) distinctions. These tend to be antipathetic to claims for universal truths, such as those generated by scientific communications and to the individualized accounts, whether emphasising personal responsibility or irresponsibility, of mental health communications. Given the social divisions which such ideological distinctions tend to produce, it is not surprising that, in the sphere of parent-child behaviour, the social disturbances which most regularly give rise to calls for action and solutions are events involving what society now defines as 'child abuse'. Once constructed, the phenomenon of child abuse both cuts across divisions of class, race and gender, to provide the notion of a universally acknowledged social problem, and at the same time gives plenty of scope for the continuation of divisions and disputes based upon what one might call the politics of difference (Dominelli, 1988; Hanmer and Statham, 1988). Issues of race, class and gender, therefore, far from disappearing, soon implant themselves and take on a new vigour within the new fields opened up by the search for and exposure of different forms of child abuse.

Meanwhile child abuse has come to be defined in increasingly wide terms, so that today it is not limited to illicit sex involving children, bodily assault and the infliction of physical and/or mental suffering. It extends also to all those occasions where what are widely recognized as fundamental individual rights are being violated.[2] Thus one can today talk of the abuse of Orkney children through their removal from their homes and their segregation and interrogation on the Scottish mainland (Asquith, 1993; Black, 1992, Clyde, 1992; King, 1995) as well as the detention of the Cleveland children in an overcrowded hospital ward (Butler-Sloss, 1988). In other words, as children are seen in Anglo-Saxon (or common law) countries as having legal rights independent of those of their parents, the violation of those rights is increasingly accepted as an abuse of the child and likely to result in harm to the child.

The overriding assumption is that child abuse, defined in such broad terms, is likely to have detrimental effects not only on the individual child victim, but also on the family. To treat child abuse as the major threat to society's efforts to reproduce its own stability and continuity has the distinct advantage of avoiding the fruitless search for empirical answers to questions that cannot be answered empirically, concerning the effects of past and present events in children's lives on their future well-being. Whatever is accepted by society as child abuse at any one time becomes in a self-evident manner damaging to the child, if not immediately, then at some time in the future when the psychological wounds are likely to open. The empirical question then becomes 'Did abuse take place?' rather than 'Was the behaviour harmful?' Attempts to identify the causes of parental failure and their real effects on children's future adulthood, the products of sociological and psychological research, lose their cogency and become irrelevant to practical policy solutions to what is seen as a matter solely of preventing and controlling the phenomenon called 'abuse'.

Moreover, the factors that might possibly affect adversely children's development into healthy adulthood are myriad, but only a small number of these become constructed by society as child abuse (King, 1995; King and Trowell, 1992). Once the problem has been constructed as child abuse, it can then be assumed that violence breeds violence and sex abuse generates sexual abusers in a circular or self-replicating way. Once the problem can be defined

in these terms, governments are faced with the task of reassuring
alarmed electorates that their policies are indeed able to break these
cycles of violence and abuse.

The increasing deployment of the criminal justice system to
identify and punish physical and sexual child abusers (Morgan and
Zedner, 1992; Wattam, 1992) and the use of public inquiries to
identify and punish violence perpetrated upon children and
families by officials (Hallett, 1989; Lee, 1980; Parton and Parton,
1989) does have the desired effect, offering some reassurance by the
setting of examples. Punishment or public humiliation, however,
can only be a provisional remedy and such punitive measures never
on their own become a satisfactory response to the long-term
problem of parental (and so family) failure, if only because
punishing parents is likely itself to result in further deprivation and
unhappiness for the child, which in turn could come to be defined
as child abuse. Indeed, convincing solutions are elusive in a
domain where official violence could be seen as just as harmful or
even more harmful to the well-being of children as the abuse
perpetrated by their parents (Asquith, 1993; Black, 1992; Butler-
Sloss, 1988; Clyde, 1992).

3.

The situation that has arisen where governments are seen as being
responsible, at least in part, for controlling the relations between
parents and their children is one of high political risk. As the recent
series of sex scandals involving politicians in Britain and the
Michael Jackson sensation in the United States have shown only too
clearly, intrusions behind the private doors of the home are likely to
be greeted with avid interest by the public. Where child abuse is
involved, they are likely to give rise to expectations that steps will
be taken not only to remedy abusive parent-child relations, but to
prevent such abuses arising in the future: an expectation that in
general terms is virtually impossible to meet. The deployment of
law with the application of its lawful/unlawful code has the
capacity to reduce the risk to manageable proportions, because
abuse, such as physical violence and aberrant sexuality within the
family, may then be seen as requiring forceful remedial action
when unlawful and only when unlawful.[3] Illegality (or unlawfulness) is necessarily defined by the law, so that legal procedures and
criteria will determine, not only which cases result in criminal
convictions or child care orders, but also which cases come to court
in the first place (King, 1995, Wattam 1992). This delegation of
responsibility by politics to law allows judicial reasoning and
government policy to claim in unison that the limits of public
responsibility are defined by the criterion of proof. If there is
inadequate evidence to prosecute or to take care proceedings, then
for the law the act is not recognizable as unlawful, while politically
it remains within the private sphere and so cannot be controlled

through direct intervention. Furthermore, this delegation also permits governments to hide behind law's immunity from responsibility for future consequences. As Niklas Luhmann tells us, in relation to child custody cases in the courts:

> Legal rules may mention future states. The prospect of the child's welfare should guide the decision about which of the divorced parents should take care of the child. *But this does not mean that the decision and all acts based on it will lose their legal validity if the future falsifies the prediction. The decision depends on present informed guesses about the future*, and legal validity is used (or misused) to absorb risks and uncertainties. (Luhmann, 1990a:234, emphasis added).

Where child abuse is alleged, if a case against parents falls short of proof for the purposes of the court, neither the law nor government may legally be held responsible for what subsequently happens to the child. The same is also true where the case is proved and subsequent events show that the child's welfare would have been better served by remaining with its parents.

From the government's perspective there is, however, a price to be paid for the deployment of the legal system. To produce laws designed to regulate politically embarrassing or disruptive social events is to draw further attention to these events as 'social problems' and to raise the expectation that solutions will be found. And so one arrives at a structural coupling and co-evolution (Luhmann, 1992a) of law and politics around events which are interpreted by both systems as child abuse.

It was fairly certain that the acclaim that greeted the Children Act 1989 in England and Wales would be followed eventually by questions as to why the Children Act is not working as well as had been predicted by its promoters and supporters. Yet, seen from the perspective of the sociological observer, such questions are based on a false premise, for neither the events themselves nor the factors which caused them to be defined as problems in the first place are likely to be changed to any degree by their re-ordering within the legal system. Where the future well-being of children is concerned, the risks and uncertainties involved in decision-making do not diminish by being situated within a comprehensive legal framework.

4.

From the perspective of politics there are other, even more serious risks in imposing upon modern liberal societies measures designed to control and eliminate child abuse and restore confidence in the family as the preferred medium for social (as well as biological) reproduction. These are the risks arising from the infringement of rights and freedoms. Governments today can ill-afford to be seen to be acting in an arbitrary or tyrannical manner, particularly in those areas of social activity which the political system has itself constructed as sacred to personal autonomy and privacy. In political terms the dilemma for governments becomes, therefore, one of balancing the effective protection of children against the rights of parents and the family to freedom from state interference (Ashenden, 1995). Seen from a sociological perspective, however, the two sides of this equation cannot be balanced in any scientifically satisfactory manner, for the one necessarily excludes the other. What we have here, in other words, is not a conflict between two interest claims, as the political formulation would have us believe, but a paradox: two incompatible statements, the one which maintains that the child must be protected, while the other defends the privacy of the family and parental autonomy against external intrusion (ibid). One is left with the result that family and parental rights are sacred, but only until such time as there are grounds for believing that a child is being abused. The way that politics resolves this seemingly paradoxical situation is by constructing agencies responsible for detecting, investigating and managing the problem of child abuse for society which supposedly have the ability to identify risk and effectively to promote children's welfare. This practical way forward creates serious tensions within child welfare agencies, for not only are their powers of identifying which of many potential risks to the child require intervention severely limited, given the contingent nature of children's development, but also the availability of what appear to be effective, or practical, ways of managing problems depends upon political and economic decisions which are far beyond their control. One alternative solution, that favoured by Brynna Kroll in this volume (pp 94-5), is to see the inner child as holding the key to the future, if only workers had the analytical skills and the time and patience to reach that elusive inner child. Another, favoured by some feminist writers, is to place the mother almost beyond criticism. Neither of these alternatives, however, is likely to satisfy the political concerns over abuse and how to prevent it.

5.

Enter the Children Act's concept of partnership or rather the implicit concept of partnership in the Children Act as elaborated by the Department of Health Guidance and Regulations (DoH 1989a, DoH 1991a, DoH 1991b, DoH 1991e, DoH 1991f) and the multitude of talks, conferences, books and articles concerned with the operation of the Act (e.g. Braye and Preston-Shoot, 1992; Buchanan, 1994; Eekelaar, 1991; Fox Harding, 1991a). The meaning of *Children Act* partnership is unclear. 'I thought I knew last week, but maybe now, you need to ask me next year', writes the editor of the recently published book, *Partnership in Practice: The Children Act 1989* (Buchanan, 1994). It is clear, however, that the concept is not used, or not used exclusively, in its business or economic form, where two or more, not necessarily equal, people or organizations, agree to embark upon a joint project or enterprise, but rather as an amorphous term, the exact meaning of which is to be determined by its context.[4]

Perhaps the best way to start the search for the meaning of partnerships involving parents is to ask in what circumstances they definitely do not occur. The term it seems, is not used to define any arrangements for the welfare of children made between parents[5] or a parent and a relative, friend, neighbour etc. regardless of the existence of oral or written agreements. Ordinary people, regardless of the closeness of their relationship to the child or sincerity of their concerns about the child's well-being, cannot form themselves into a partnership in any way that is recognized by the Department of Health. This may be an obvious point, but it needs to be stated.

The Children Act and accompanying Rules, Regulations, Guidance etc. may therefore be seen as constructing the notion of partnership in such a way as to require the participation of some official person, authorized by reason of his or her qualifications or status to enter into partnerships for the protection of children or the promotion of their welfare. Most often, this official will be a local authority social worker. This idiosyncratic version of partnership, it must be emphasised, is not a construction of law but rather of politics, in the sense that it sets up the framework, not of legal relations, but of power relations between officials and parents or care-givers.

To appreciate the importance of this device for politics and thus for government, we need to refer to our earlier discussion of the paradox of child protection and respect for parental rights. Seen in the light of these seemingly incompatible objectives, what the notion of partnership does is to allow officials to intrude upon the privacy of family life, while maintaining intact the structure of parental and family rights.[6] Instead of trampling on the sacred ground of family life, the social worker takes on the status of a third parent, or, in the case of single-parent families, a second or substitute parent, involved with the other parent in a joint enterprise to promote the child's welfare.[7] This is not to suggest in any way that partnership arrangements are necessarily one-sided. The agreements may well place parents or other care-givers in a better position to secure support and services for themselves and for the child than might have been the case if the responsibilities to the social services department had not been specified in a semi-formal manner.

It hardly needs to be stated, however, that local authority social service departments charged by government with the protection of children have much to gain from entering into partnership arrangements with parents. Partnership operates for them as an observation post sited in the midst of family life from where, under ideal conditions, all the activities of the family may be noted, and reported back to case conferences and planning meetings. Partnership then allows the social worker to play the part of an ethologist, while leaving the political environment, the delicate balance between family and state, between private and public, largely undisturbed.

6.

So we come to law. To obtain an order under the Children Act, local authorities not only have to prove that abuse is occurring, but they also have to show that the 'significant harm, or the likelihood of harm, is attributable to care given to the child, or likely to be given to him if the order were not made'[8]. The question as to whether parents are both willing and capable of co-operating voluntarily with social workers so as to ensure the safety of the child becomes, therefore a crucial issue for law. In law's coding of the situation, 'partnership failure' becomes a significant event by precluding arguments 'that the parents can be trusted to work in unison with social workers concerned for the child's future safety. It becomes, in effect, a pre-coding for law, avoiding the necessity of undertaking the complex and lengthy task of examining the intelligence, integrity and personalities of the parents. Partnership failure speaks for itself. Braye and Preston-Shoot draw attention to concern among social work practitioners 'about setting people up to fail making it difficult to retain involvement after such "failure" ' (Braye and Preston-Shoot 1992:513). They do not recognize, however, that the practitioners have themselves been 'set up' by law as agents for identifying parental failure.

This does not mean to say that in every situation where partnership can be shown to have failed, the courts are bound to make an order. The parents may be able to show, for example, that their behaviour was misinterpreted as indicating failure, that exceptional circumstances caused the failure or that any failure was due to the local authority's incompetence in carrying out their side of the agreement. The point is that, whatever the original intention of the policy makers and social service administrators, the continuing existence of partnership inevitably becomes reconstructed by law as an indicating the presence of 'lawfulness' in the relationship between the family and the child protection agency, while its failure raises the presumption that the situation has become 'unlawful'.

Once legal proceedings have been started, parents may well take the view that partnership has operated more as a cloak to conceal the true intentions of social workers than as a structure to promote co-operation and joint enterprises, for all the information that the social services and other agencies acquired during the partnership is now reproduced in court in the form of evidence that the child is being abused or neglected.

The law resolves the paradox of child protection and children's rights by introducing a distinction based on the availability or otherwise of evidence or proof. To quote Lord Justice Butler-Sloss (1993), the chairperson of the Cleveland inquiry, in a speech she gave advising social workers on what criteria they should apply in deciding whether to remove children,

> there are children who have been abused and you can prove it, and those children sooner or later you will be taking away from home, unless you can produce a good system of protection for them in their own home. Then there are children who haven't been abused – you have to be careful that you recognise they have rights. Then there are also the children who may have been abused and you can't prove it ... but a solid, calm assessment that you can't prove the allegation and you won't be helping the child in such a case by taking it away from home and sending him back again. (pp.55-6)

Within law, therefore, privacy, freedoms and rights are only conditional and may be intruded upon and overridden provided that social workers have the proof or honestly believe that they are able to prove that the child is being abused. Proof or belief in proof is sufficient under the Children Act for the state to intervene through an Emergency Protection or a Child Assessment Order. The liberal principles of privacy, freedom and autonomy which within the sphere of political communication parents are supposed to enjoy, do not, however, disappear altogether. Instead, they are reconstructed by law as procedural rights. It is here that law on its home ground is able to offer the parents a panoply of safeguards against arbitrary or unfair decisions.

For the former partners the issue is thus transformed from one of co-operation in the promotion of the child's welfare to that, on the one side, of proving abuse according to fairly strict rules of evidence and procedure and, on the other side, of using the procedural safeguards and deploying legal skills and arguments in an effort to prevent the court from deciding that an order is justified.

In this situation any talk of a continuing partnership would be quite out of place. It would be ludicrous to suggest that a partnership existed between court, parents and social workers to protect the child. The settlements that are forged together outside the courtroom to avoid the risks and the cost of fighting the case in court and then approved by the judge are not partnership agreements. Unlike in other jurisdictions, a judge in English law cannot be constructed as a partner; judges cannot negotiate or enter into joint enterprises with litigants. Within law, liberal order, the protection of the citizen's privacy and freedom, depends upon the impartiality, independence and aloofness of the judge.

For those social workers, and child welfare experts who had expected the court to do no more than reprimand parents for their breach of the agreement and give them a stiff warning of the likely consequences of future failures, the court experience can be very frustrating. To present legal decision-making as no more than a stage in the continuing process of protecting the child is to misunderstand the autopoietic nature of law[9] and the role that law plays in a society which places a high value on the maintenance of liberal order. While the device of partnership may have lowered the barriers between public and private, law raises them again, but in doing so, transforms them into procedural obstacles and evidentiary requirements which must be overcome before any order may be made to protect the child. On the other hand, to accept law's definition of the situation as one where parental illegality must be proved and partnerships must be shown to have failed is to ignore or, at least, to discount for the time being, the strong possibility that even after the court case is over, the child will remain with or be returned to the parents and that new partnerships will need to be forged, if the child is to be adequately protected.

7.

For politics to give law a leading role in the regeneration of society through the family by expecting law to solve the problems associated with the risks involved in resolving the paradox of child protection and family rights, is itself a risky strategy. Law's only way of providing apparent resolutions to paradoxes is by transforming them into legal distinctions. Within law, therefore, just as the notion of 'the needs of the child' becomes transformed into issues of the existence of sufficient proof and evidence, so the notion of partnership is reconstructed in terms of parental competence and incompetence, responsibility and irresponsibility.

The effects of such reconstructions are not unfortunately localised or limited to the activities of lawyers within the confines of the court. The dominant role given to law by the Children Act 1989 in reconciling the irreconcilable through the production of measures designed to protect children and promote their welfare, has the result of obliging other social systems to adopt law's distinctions in their own communications and operations. It is no surprise, therefore, to see social service managers using partnership from the outset, not so much as a vehicle for joint enterprise, but rather as a device for obtaining evidence and proving parental incompetence and irresponsibility in court, should things go wrong.

Notes

1. This was the main function of the wardship jurisdiction throughout the 18th and most of the 19th centuries. Blackstone in his 1765 Commentaries on the Laws of England wrote,

    The power of a parent by our English laws is ... sufficient to keep the child in order and obedience. He may lawfully correct his child, being under age, in any reasonable manner; for this is for the benefit of his education. The consent or concurrence of the parent to the marriage of his child under age ...

is now absolutely necessary; for without it the contract is void. And this also is another means, which the law has put into the parent's hands, in order the better to discharge his duty; first, of protecting his children from the snares of artful and designing persons; and next, of settling them properly in life, by preventing the ill consequences of too early and precipitate marriages.

2. Examples would be the detention of children without judicial authority or the refusal or withholding of life-saving medical treatment.
3. This does not necessarily mean that it is a crime, but that it falls on the wrong side of the line which divides legally justifiable and legally unjustifiable behaviour towards children.
4. See Judith Masson chapter 2 in this volume p.21.
5. It is true that Christine Piper's chapter in this book deals with the situation of partnership between parents, but at the level of social communication these arrangements are rarely, if ever, described as 'partnerships'.
6. This is very similar to the requirement that French children's judges secure wherever possible the co-operation of the family, before making any order in respect of the child.
7. Reminiscent of the state paternalism which finds expression, according to Jacques Donzelot, in the judge taking over the responsibilities, traditionally those of the father, as head of the family. See Donzelot (1980).
8. Section 31(2).
9. For discussions of autopoietic law see Luhmann (1992b); King (1993) and Teubner (1993).

Bibliography

Advisory Centre for Education (1992) 'Who is a Parent?' *ACE Bulletin*, May-June, 5

Aldgate J. (1988) 'Work with Children Experiencing Separation and Loss: A Theoretical Framework' in J. Aldgate and J. Simmonds (eds) (1988)

Aldgate J. and Simmonds J. (eds) (1988) *Direct Work with Children: A Guide for Social Work Practitioners* London: Batsford Academic

Aldgate J. (1991) 'Partnership with Parents: Fantasy or Reality?' *Adoption & Fostering* 5

Aldgate J., Tunstall J. and McBeath G. (1992) *National Monitoring of the Children Act: Part III section 17 – the First Year* Oxford University/NCVCCO

Aldgate J., Heath A., Colton M. and Simm M. (1993) 'Social Work and the Education of Children in Foster Care' *Adoption and Fostering* 25-34

Archer L. and Whitaker D. (1992) 'Decisions, Tasks and Uncertainties in Child Protection Work' *Journal of Social Work Practice* 63

Armstrong H. (1993) *Report of the Area Children Protection Committee Conferences 1992-3* London: Department of Health

Ashenden S. (1995) 'Political Rationality and Child Sexuality' in (eds) Barry, A., Rose N., and Bell, V. *Foucault and Politics: Liberalism, Neo-Liberalism and the Rationality of Government* London:UCL Press

Asquith S. (1993) *Protecting Children. Cleveland to Orkney. More Lessons to Learn* Edinburgh: HMSO

Atherton C. 'Client Participation in Decision-Making Meetings' in (eds) Family Rights Group *The Children Act 1989: Working in Partnership with Families. Reader* 183. London: HMSO

Audit Commission (1989) *Housing the Homeless: the Local Authority Role* London: HMSO

Audit Commission (1992) *Getting In on The Act* London: HMSO

Audit Commission (1993) *Children First – A Study of Hospital Services* London: HMSO

Axline V. M. (1964) *Dibs – In Search of Self* Harmondsworth: Penguin

Bainham A. (1990a) 'The Children Act 1989: Parenthood and Guardianship' *Family Law* 192

Bainham A. (1990b) 'The Children Act 1989: The State and the Family' *Family Law* 231

Bainham A. (1990c) 'The Privatisation of the Public Interest in Children' *Modern Law Review* 206-221

Bainham A. (1990d) 'The Children Act 1989: Welfare and Non-Interventionism' *Family Law* 143

Bala N. (1991) 'An Introduction to Child Protection Problems' in (eds) Bala N., Hornick J. and Vogl R. *Canadian Child Welfare Law* Toronto: Thompson

Bannister J. (1993) *Homeless Young People in Scotland* Edinburgh: HMSO

Barclay Report (1982) *Social Workers, Their Roles and Tasks* London: Bedford Square Press

Barnhorst N. and Walter B. (1991) 'Child Protection Legislation in Canada' in (eds) Bala N., Hornick J. and Vogl R. *Canadian Child Welfare Law* Toronto: Thompson

Bastiani J. (1993) 'Parents as Partners; Genuine Progress or Empty Rhetoric?' in Munn P. (ed) *Parents and Schools: Customers, Managers or Partners?* London: Routledge

Bell M. and Daly R. 'Social Workers and Solicitors: Working Together' (1992) *Family Law* 257

Bick E. (1964) 'Notes on Infant Observation in Psychoanalytic Training' in *International Journal of Psychoanalysis* No. 45: 558-566

Bion W. (1959) 'Attacks on Linking' in *International Journal of Psychoanalysis* 40: 308-15

Bion W. (1962) *Learning from Experience* London: Heinemann

Biehal N. and Sainsbury E. (1991) 'From Values to Rights in Social Work' 21 *Brit J of Social Work* 248

Black R. (1992) *'Orkney, A Place of Safety?'* Edinburgh: Canongate Press

Bowlby J. (1969) *Attachment* London: Hogarth Press

Bowlby J. (1973) *Loss: Sadness and Depression* London: Hogarth Press

Brandon M. (1992) 'Anticipating the Impact of the Children Act on Social Work Practice in Child Care' *Adoption and Fostering* 22-9

Braun D. (1992) 'Working with Parents' in (ed) G. Pugh *Contemporary Issues in the Early Years: Working Collaboratively For Children* London: National Children's Bureau

Braye S. and Preston-Shoot M. (1992) 'Honourable Intentions: Partnership and Written Agreements in Welfare Legislation' *Journal of Social Welfare and Family Law* 511

Braye S. and Preston-Shoot M. (1994) 'Partners in Community Care? Rethinking the Relationship Between the Law and Social Work Practice' *Journal of Social Welfare and Family Law* 163

Brophy J. (1994) 'Parent Management Committees and Pre-School Playgroups: The Partnership Model and Future Management Policy' *Journal of Social Policy* 161-194

Brophy J. and Smart C. (eds) (1985) *Women in Law* London: Routledge & Kegan Paul

Buchanan A. (1993) *Partnership in Practice: The Children Act 1989* Aldershot: Avebury

Butler, et al. (1993) 'The Children Act 1989 and the Unmarried Father' *Journal of Child Law* 157

Butler-Sloss L. J. (1993) 'From Cleveland to Orkney' in (ed) S. Asquith *Protecting Children. Cleveland to Orkney. More Lessons to Learn* Edinburgh: HMSO

Butler-Sloss L. J. (1988) *Report of the Inquiry into Child Abuse in Cleveland* London: H.M.S.O

Calasanti T. and Bailey C. (1991) 'Gender Inequality and the Division of Household Labor in the United States and Sweden. A Socialist Feminist Approach' *Social Problems* 34

Cannan C. (1992) *Changing Families Changing Welfare* Hemel Hempstead: Harvester Wheatseaf

Central Advisory Council for Education (England) (1967) *Children and Their Primary Schools* (Plowden Report), London: HMSO

CCETSW (1991) Paper 30, *Dip SW: Rules and Requirements for the Diploma in Social Work* (2nd Edition) London: CCETSW

Clulow C. and Vincent C. (1987) *In The Child's Best Interests* London: Tavistock/Sweet and Maxwell

Clyde L. (1992) *The Report of the Inquiry into the Removal of Children from Orkney in February 1991* Edinburgh: HMSO

Connolly M. (1994) 'An Act of Empowerment: The Children, Young Persons and Their Families Act (1989)' 24 *Br J. of Social Work* 87-100

David M. (1985) 'Motherhood and Social Policy: A Matter of Education?' *Critical Social Policy* 28-48

David M. (1991a) 'A Gender Agenda: Women and Family in the New ERA?' *British Journal of Sociology of Education* 433

David M. (1991b) 'Putting on an Act for Children' in (eds) Maclean M. and Groves D. *Women's Issues in Social Policy* London: Routledge

David M. (1993) *Parents, Gender and Education Reform* Cambridge: Polity Press

David M., Edwards R., Hughes M. and Ribbens J. (1993) *Mothers in Education: Inside Out? Exploring Family-Education Policy and Experience* London: Macmillan

Davidson R. (1980) 'Restoring Children to Their Families' in Triseliotis, J. (ed.) *New Directions in Foster Care and Adoption*

Davis G. and Bader K. (1985) 'In-Court Mediation: The Consumer View I and II' *Family Law* 42-9 and 82-6

Davis G., Macleod A. and Murch M. (1983) 'Undefended Divorce: Should s41 of the MCA be Repealed?' *Modern Law Review* 121

Department of Education and Science (1990) *Starting With Quality: the report of the committee of enquiry into the quality of educational experience offered to 3 and 4 year olds* London: HMSO

Department of Education and Science (1991) *The Parents' Charter* London: HMSO

Department of Education and Science (1992) *The Parents' Charter – Children with Special Needs,* London: HMSO

DFE (Department for Education) (1994) *Our Children's Education, The Updated Parents' Charter* London: HMSO

Department of the Environment/Department of Health/Welsh

Office (1991) *Homelessness Code of Guidance for Local Authorities* (3rd Edition) London: HMSO

Department of Health and Social Security (1985) *Place of Safety and Interim Care Orders, Review of Child Care Law* London: HMSO.

Department of Health and Social Security (1987) *The Law on Child Care and Family Services* London: HMSO

Department of Health and Social Security (1988) *Working Together: A Guide to Arrangements for Inter-Agency Co-operation for the Protection of Children from Abuse* London: HMSO

Department of Health (1989a) *The Care of Children. Principles and Practice in Regulations and Guidance* London: HMSO

Department of Health (1989b) *An Introduction to the Children Act 1989* London: HMSO

Department of Health (1990) *The Care of Children: Principles and Practice in Regulations and Guidance* London: HMSO

Department of Health (1991a) *Care Management and Assessment. Practitioners' Guidance* London: HMSO

Department of Health (1991b) *Care Management and Assessment. Summary of Practice Guidance* London: HMSO

Department of Health (1991c) *Child Abuse: A Study of Enquiry Reports 1980-1989* London: HMSO

Department of Health (1991d) *The Children Act 1989 Guidance and Regulations, Volume 1, Court Orders* London: HMSO

Department of Health (1991e) *The Children Act 1989: Guidance and Regulations, Volume 2, Family Support, Day Care and Educational Provision for Young People* London: HMSO

Department of Health (1991f) *The Children Act 1989: Guidance and Regulations, Volume 3, Family Placements* London: HMSO

Department of Health (1991g) *Patterns and Outcomes in Child Placement* London: HMSO

Department of Health (1991h) *Welfare of Children and Young People in Hospital* London: HMSO

Department of Health (1991i) *Working Together under the Children Act 1989* London: HMSO

Department of Health/Welsh Office (1992) *Children Act Report 1992* Cm. 2144 London: HMSO

Department of Health (1993a) *Report to the Secretary of State on the Children Act 1989* London: HMSO

Department of Health (1993b) *Children and Young People on Child Protection Registers, 1992* London: HMSO

Department of Health (1993c) *London Boroughs and English Authorities Area Child Protection Committee Reports April 1990 – March 1992* London: HMSO

Department of Health (1994) *Children and Young People on Child Protection Registers: Year Ending 31 March 1993* London: HMSO

De Young M. (1994) 'Women as Mothers and Wives in Paternally

Incestuous Families: Coping with Role Conflict' *Child Abuse and Neglect* 73-83

Dewar J. (1992) *Law and the Family* London: Butterworths

Di Leo J. (1979) *Young Children and Their Drawings* London: Constable

Dominelli L. (1988) *Anti-Racist Social Work* London: MacMillan

Douglas G. (1990) 'Family Law Under the Thatcher Government' *Journal of Law and Society* 411

Donzelot J. (1980) *The Policing of Families: Welfare Versus the State* London: Hutchinson

Edgell S. (1980) *Middle Class Couples: A Study of Segregation, Domination and Inequality in Marriage* London: Allen and Unwin

Edwards S. and Halpern A. (1992) 'Parental Responsibility, An Instrument of Social Policy' *Family Law* 113

Eekelaar J. (1991) 'Parental Responsibility: State of Nature or Nature of the State?' *Journal of Social Welfare and Family Law* 37

Elliot J. et al. (1981) *School Accountability* London: Grant McIntyre

Erikson E. H. (1965) *Childhood and Society* Harmondsworth: Penguin

Fahlberg V. (1982) *Child Development* British Association for Adoption and Fostering

Family Rights Group (1991) 'Written Agreements' in (eds) Family Rights Group *The Children Act 1989: Working in Partnership with Families. Reader* 261 London: HMSO

Farmer E., Owen M. and Parker R. (1993) *Decision-making, Intervention and Outcome in Child Protection Work* Bristol: University of Bristol

Farmer E. and Owen M. (Forthcoming) *Decision-making, Intervention and Outcome in Child Protection Work*, London: HMSO

Finch J. (1984) 'The Deceit of Self-Help: Pre-School Playgroups and Working Class Mothers' *J. of Social Policy* 1-20

Fineman M. (1991) *The Illusion of Equality* London and Chicago: University of Chicago Press

Fisher M., Marsh P. and Phillips D., (1986) *In and out of Care* London: Batsford

Fox-Harding L. M. (1991a) 'The Children Act in Context: Four Perspectives in Child Care Law and Policy (1) and (2)' *Journal of Social Welfare and Family Law* 179 and 285

Fox-Harding L. (1991b) *Perspectives in Child Care Policy* Harlow: Longman

Fox I. (1985) *Private Schools and Public Issues: The Parents' Views* London: Macmillan

Freeman M.D.A . (1992) *Children, Their Families and the Law* London: BASW, Macmillan

Freud S. (1905) *Three Essays on the Theory of Sexuality* in Freud S., Strachey J. and Freud A. *The Complete Psychological Works of*

Sigmund Freud Vol. 7 Hogarth Press and Institute of Psycho-analysis: London

Frothingham T.E., Barnett R.A.M., Hobbs C.J. and Wynne J.M. (1993) 'Child Sexual Abuse in Leeds Before and After Cleveland' *Child Abuse Rev* 23

Frug M. J. (1992) *Postmodern Legal Feminism* London: Routledge

Furniss T. (1991) *The Multi-professional Handbook of Child Sexual Abuse* London: Routledge

Galanter M. (1974) 'Why the "Haves" Come Out Ahead: Speculation on the Limits of Legal Change' *Law and Society Review* 95

Gerlis S. (1994) 'Talking Shop: Head Banging' *Family Law* 154

Gibbons J., Conroy S. and Bell C., (Forthcoming) *Operation of Child Protection Registers* London: HMSO

Greif G. (1992) 'Lone Fathers in the United States: An Overview and Practice Implications' *Brit. J. Social Work* 565-574

Gusfield J. R. (1973) *Symbolic Crusade: Status Politics and the American Temperance Movement* London: Urbana, University of Illinois Press

Hadfield B. and Lavery R. (1991) 'Public and Private Law Controls on Decision-Making for Children' *Journal of Social Welfare and Family Law* 454

Hallett C. (1989) 'Child Abuse Inquiries and Public Policy' in (ed.) Stevenson O. *Child Abuse: Public Policy and Professional Practice* Hemel-Hempstead: Harvester-Wheatsheaf

Hanmer J. and Statham D. (1988) *Women and Social Work: Towards a Woman Centred Practice* London: Macmillan

Harris N. (1992) 'The Children Act 1989: Parental Responsibility and Decisions Concerning a Child's Education' *Education and the Law* 1

Harris N. and Van Bijsterfeld S. (1993) 'Parents as "Consumers" of Education in England and Wales and the Netherlands: A Comparative Analysis' *Int. J. of Law and the Family* 178-204

Harris R. and Webb D. (1987) *Welfare, Power, and Juvenile Justice: The Social Control of Delinquent Youth* London: Tavistock Publications

Harrison C. and Masson J. (1994) 'Working in Partnership with "Lost" Parents: Issues of Theory and Practice' *Adoption and Fostering* 40-44

Harwin J. (1992) 'Child Protection and the Role of the Social Worker Under the Children Act 1989' in (ed) Parry M. *The Children Act 1989: Conflict and Compromise* Hull: Hull University Law School

Herbert E. and Carpenter B. (1994) 'Fathers – The Secondary Partners:
Professional Perceptions and Fathers' Reflections' *Children and Society* 31-41

Hodges S. (1994) *Has the Children Act had any Effect on the Work of Clinical and Educational Psychologists? – An Exploratory Survey* Dissertation – Masters Degree in Clinical Psychology, University of East London (unpublished)

Home Office/Department of Health (1992) *Video Recorded Testimony. Memorandum of Good Practice* London: HMSO

Hooper C. (1992) 'Child Sexual Abuse: Variations on a Theme' in (ed) Smart C. *Regulating Womanhood* London: Routledge

Howe D. (1992) 'Theories of Helping, Empowerment and Participation' in (ed) Thoburn, J. *Participation in Practice: Involving Families in Child Protection* Norwich: University of East Anglia

Isaac B. (1991) 'Negotiation in Partnership Work' in (eds) Family Rights Group *The Children Act 1989: Working in Partnership with Families. Reader* 201 London: HMSO

Jarman M. (1993) 'Contracting: Opportunity or Threat?' *Children & Society* 331

Jenkins J. (1991) 'Inter-Agency Issues' in (eds) Family Rights Group *The Children Act 1989: Working in Partnership with Families. Reader* 227 London: HMSO

Jewett C. (1984) *Helping Children Cope with Separation and Loss* London: Batsford Academic/BAAF

Johnson D. (1987) *Private Schools and State Schools: Two Systems or One?* Milton Keynes: Open University Press

Kaganas F. (28 Oct 1993) 'Unequal Balance' *Community Care. Inside* 1

Kaganas F. and Piper C. (1994) 'Joint Parenting Under the Children Act 1989' in Lockton, D. (ed.) *Children and the Law* London: Cavendish Publications

Kimmelman E. (1985) *No Quiet Place*, Review Committee on Indian and Metis Adoptions and Placements, Winnipeg: Manitoba Department of Community Services

King M. (1987) 'Playing the Symbols: Custody and the Law Commission' *Family Law* 186-91

King M. (1993) 'The "Truth" about Autopoiesis' *Journal of Law and Society* 1

King M. (1995, forthcoming) 'Law's Healing of Children's Hearings. The Paradox Moves North' *Journal of Social Policy*

King M. and Trowell J. (1992) *Children's Welfare and the Law. The Limits of Legal Intervention* London: Sage

Kirwan M. (1994) 'Gender and Social Work: Will Dip.S.W. Make a Difference?' *Br. J Social Work* 137-155

Klein M. (1926) 'The Psychological Principles of Infant Analysis' in (ed) Mitchell J. (1986) *The Selected Melanie Klein* Harmondsworth: Penguin

Klein M. (1932) *The Psychoanalysis of Children*, London: Hogarth Press

Klein M. (1940) *Mourning – Its Relation to Manic Depressive States* in (ed) Mitchell J. (1986) *The Selected Melanie Klein* Harmondsworth: Penguin

Klein M. (1952) *On Observing the Behaviour of Young Infants* in Klein M. and Riviere J. *Developments in Psychoanalysis* London: Hogarth Press

Klein M . (1955) *The Psychoanalytic Play Technique: Its History and Significance* in (ed) Mitchell J. (1986) *The Selected Melanie Klein* Harmondsworth: Penguin

Klein M. (1957) *Envy and Gratitude: A Study of Unconscious Sources* London: Tavistock

Klein M. (1961) *Narrative of a Child Analysis* London: Hogarth Press

Klein M. (1963) *Our Adult World and Its Roots in Infancy and Other Essays* London: Heinemann

Kline M. (1992) 'Child Welfare Law "Best Interests of the Child" Ideology and the First Nations' 375 *Osgoode Hall Law Journal*

Kline P. (1984) *Psychology and Freudian Theory: An Introduction* London: Methuen

Kroll B. (1994) *Chasing Rainbows: Children,Divorce and Loss* London: Russell House Publishing

Langam M. and Day L. (1992) *Women, Oppression and Social Work* London: Routledge

Law Commission (1986) *Family Law, Review of Child Law: Custody, Working Paper No. 96* London: HMSO

Law Commission (1988) *Family Law, Review of Child Law: Guardianship and Custody, No. 172* London: HMSO

Lee C. (1980) 'Official Inquiries' in (ed) Carver V. *Child Abuse. A Study Text* Milton Keynes: Open University Press

Legal Aid HandBook (1992) London: Sweet and Maxwell

Lehner L. (1994) 'Education for Parents Divorcing in California' *Family and Conciliation Courts Review* 50

Lewis A. (1992) 'The Background to Working in Partnership' in Lewis et al *Participation in Practice: Training Pack* Norwich: University of East Anglia

Lewis A., Thoburn J. and Shemmings D. (1992) *Participation in Practice: Training Pack* Norwich: University of East Anglia

Lieberman F. (1979) *Social Work with Children* Human Sciences Press

London Borough of Brent (1985) *A Child in Trust: Report of the Panel of Inquiry Investigating the Circumstances Surrounding the Death of Jasmine Beckford* London: London Borough of Brent

London Borough of Lambeth (1987) *Whose Child? The Report of the Public Inquiry in the Death of Tyra Henry* London: London Borough of Lambeth

Lord Chancellor's Department (1993) *Looking to the Future: Mediation and the Ground for Divorce* London: HMSO

Luhmann N. (1976) 'The Future Cannot Begin: Temporal Structures in Modern Society' *Social Research* 130

Luhmann N. (1977) 'Differentiation of Society' *Canadian Journal of Sociology* 29

Luhmann N. (1986a) 'The Autopoiesis of Social Systems' in (eds) Geyer F. and van der Zouwen J. *Sociocybernetic Paradoxes: Observation, Control and Evolution of Self-Steering Systems* London: Beverly Hills

Luhmann N. (1986b) 'Theory of Social Systems and Epistomology' *Philosophy of the Social Sciences* 112

Luhmann N. (1988) 'Closure and Openness: On the Reality in the World of Law' in (ed.) Teubner G. *Autopoietic Law. A New Approach to Law and Society* Berlin and New York: De Gruyter

Luhmann N. (1990a) *Essays on Self Reference* New York: Columbia University Press

Luhmann N. (1990b) *Political Theory in the Welfare State* Berlin and New York: Walter de Gruyter

Luhmann N. (1992a) 'Operational Closure and Structural Coupling' *Cardozo Law Review* 1419-1441

Luhmann N. (1992b) 'Some Problems with "Reflexive Law" ' in (eds) Teubner G. and Febbrajo A. *European Yearbook of the Sociology of Law* Milan: Guiffrè

Maccoby E. and Mnookin R. (1992) *Dividing the Child: Social and Legal Dilemmas of Custody* Harvard: Harvard University Press

Marsh P. (1990) 'Changing Practice in Child Care – The Children Act 1989' *Adoption and Fostering* 27-30

McGregor O. (1957) *Divorce in England* London: Heinemann

Menzies I. (1970) *The Functioning of Social Systems As A Defence Against Anxiety* London: Tavistock Publications

Miller A. (1987) *The Drama of Being A Child* London: Virago

Miller J. (1992) *More has Meant Women: The Feminisation of Schooling* London: University of London, Tufnell Press

Miller L., Rustin M., Rustin M. and Shuttleworth J. (1989) (eds) *Closely Observed Infants* London: Duckworth

Millham S. et al (1989) *Access Disputes in Child Care* Aldershot: Gower

Milner J. (1993) 'A Disappearing Act: The Differing Career Paths of Fathers and Mothers in Child Protection Investigations' *Critical Social Policy* 48

Mitchell J. (ed.) (1986) *The Selected Melanie Klein* Harmondsworth: Penguin

Montgomery J. (1993) 'Consent to Health Care for Children' *Journal of Child Law* 117

Monture P. (1989) 'A Vicious Circle: Child Welfare and the First Nations' *Canadian Journal of Women and the Law* 1

Morgan J. and Zedner L. (1992) *Child Victims. Crime, Impact and Criminal Justice* Oxford: Clarendon Press

Murch M. (1980) *Justice, Welfare and Divorce* London: Sweet and Maxwell

Neary V. (26 Sept 1991) 'Mrs. Brown's Bad Days' *Community Care. Inside* ii

Neate P. (12 Dec, 1991) 'Pulling in Different Directions' *Community Care* 12

Nelken D. (1987) 'The Use of "Contracts" as a Social Work Technique' *Current Legal Problems* 207

Nelken D. (1988) 'Social Work Contracts and Social Control' in (ed.)

Matthews R. *Informal Justice?* London: Sage

Niner P. (1989) *Homelessness in Nine Local Authorities: Case Studies of Policy and Practice* Department of the Environment, London: HMSO

Oaklander V. (1978) *Windows to Our Children* Real People Press

O'Donovan K. (1985) *Sexual Divisions in Law* London: Weidenfeld and Nicholson

Open University (1991) *The Children Act 1989: A Guide for the Education Service* Milton Keynes: Open University Press

Packman J., Randall J. and Jacques N. (1986) *Who Needs Care?* Oxford: Blackwell

Parry M. (1992) 'The Children Act 1989: A Conflict of Ideologies' in (ed.) Parry M. *The Children Act 1989: Conflict and Compromise* Hull: Hull University Law School

Partington J. and Wragg T. (1989) *Schools and Parents* London: Cassell

Parton C. (1990) 'Women, Gender Oppression and Child Abuse' in *Taking Child Abuse Seriously* The Violence Against Children Study Group: Unwin Hyman

Parton N. (1979) 'The Natural History of Child Abuse: A Study in Problem Definition' *British Journal of Social Work* 9, 4: 427-51

Parton N. (1991) *Governing the Family – Child Care, Child Protection and the State* London: Macmillan

Parton N. and Parton C. (1989) 'The Law and Dangerousness' in (ed.) Stevenson O. *Child Abuse: Public Policy and Professional Practice* Hemel-Hempstead: Harvester-Wheatsheaf

Pearson J. (1993) 'Ten Myths About Family Law' *Family Law Quarterly* 279

Petersen V. and Steinman S. (1994) 'Helping Children Succeed After Divorce: A Court Mandated Educational Programme for Divorcing Parents' *Family and Conciliation Courts Review* 27

Phillips M. (1993) 'Ninety Minutes to Lose a Daughter' *The Guardian* 13th February

Piaget J. (1969) *The Psychology of the Child* London: Routledge and Kegan Paul

Piper C. (1988) 'Divorce Conciliation in the UK: How Responsible are Parents?' *International Journal of Sociology of Law* 477

Piper C. (1993) *The Responsible Parent: A Study of Divorce Mediation* Hemel Hempstead: Harvester Wheatsheaf

Piper C. (1994a) 'Looking to the Future for Children' *Journal of Child Law* 99

Piper C. (1994b) 'Parental Responsibility and the Education Acts' *Family Law* 146

Pugh G. (1983) 'Parental Involvement in Schooling: A Review of Research' *National Childrens Bureau Highlight* London: National Children's Bureau

Pugh G. (1985) 'Parents & Professionals in Partnership: Issues & Implications' *Partnership Paper No. 2* National Children's Bureau

Report of the Aboriginal Justice Inquiry of Manitoba (1991) *The Justice System and Aboriginal People* Winnipeg: The Province of Manitoba

Report of the Committee on Child Health Services (1976) *Fit for the Future*

Report of the Matrimonial Causes Procedure Committee (1985) London: HMSO

Rochdale Area Child Protection Committee (1993) *Parental Participation in Child Protection Conferences* Cheshire: Impact Performance Management Consultancy

Roche J. (1991) 'The Children Act 1989: Once a Parent Always a Parent?' *Journal of Social Welfare and Family Law* 345-61

Rojek C. and Collins S (1987) 'Contract or Con Trick?' *British Journal of Social Work* 199

Rojek C., Peacock G. and Collins S. (1988) *Social Work and Received Ideas* London: Routledge and Kegan Paul

Ryan M. (1991) 'Procedures for Representations and Complaints' in (eds) Family Rights Group *The Children Act 1989: Working in Partnership with Families. Reader* 167 London: HMSO

Ryburn M. (1991a) 'Empowering Clients' in (eds) Family Rights Group *The Children Act 1989: Working in Partnership with Families. Reader* 13 London: HMSO

Ryburn M. (1991b) 'The Children Act – Power and Empowerment' *Adoption and Fostering* 10

Salzberger-Wittenberg I. (1970) *Psychoanalytic Insight and Relationships: A Kleinian Approach* Routledge Kegan Paul

Scott G. (1990) 'Parents and Pre-School Services: Issues of Parental Involvement' *International Journal of Sociology and Social Policy* 1

Secretary of State for Social Services (1988) *Report of the Inquiry into Child Abuse in Cleveland* London: HMSO

Sheridan M. (1968) *The Developmental Progress of Infants and Young Children* (Second Edition) London: HMSO

Sheridan M. (1992) *From Birth to Five Years: Children's Developmental Progress* London: Routledge

Sinclair, Judge M., Phillips D. and Bala N. (1991) 'Aboriginal Child Welfare in Canada' in (eds) Bala N., Hornick J. and Vogl R. *Canadian Child Welfare Law* Toronto: Thompson

Smith E. C. (1984) 'Joint Custody: The View from the Bench' *Michigan Bar Journal* 155

Smith R. (1991) 'Child Care: Welfare, Protection or Rights?' *Journal of Social Welfare and Family Law* 469

Smith V. (1993) 'Part 1 Section 8 Care Orders – Can They Exist?' *Family Law* 645

Social Services Inspectorate (1990) *Child Care Policy: Putting it in Writing* London: HMSO

Staines D. (26 Sept. 1991) 'The Dawning of a New Era' *Community Care. Inside* i

Storr A. (1989) *Freud* Oxford: Oxford University Press

Teubner G. (1993) *Law as an Autopoietic System* Oxford: Blackwell

The Law on Child Care and Family Services (1987) cm 62, London: HMSO

Thoburn J. (1991a) 'The Children Act 1989; Balancing Child Welfare with the Concept of Partnership with Parents' *Journal of Social Welfare and Family Law* 331

Thoburn J. (1991b) 'Partnership and Compulsion' in (eds) Family Rights Group *The Children Act 1989: Working in Partnership with Families. Reader* 107 London: HMSO

Thoburn J. (1992) ' "Working Together" and Parental Attendances at Case Conferences' *Journal of Child Law* 11

Thoburn J., Lewis A and Shemmings D. (1995) *Paternalism or Partnership? The Involvement of Family Members in Child Protection* London: HMSO

Thompson D. A. R. (1988) 'Taking Children and Facts Seriously: Evidence Law in Child Protection Proceedings – Part I' *Canadian Journal of Family Law* 11

Thompson D. A. R. (1989a) 'Taking Children and Facts Seriously: Evidence Law in Child Protection Proceedings – Part II' *Canadian Journal of Family Law* 213

Thompson D. A. R. (1989b) 'Why Hasn't the Charter Mattered in Child Protection' *Canadian Journal of Family Law* 133

Thompson L. and Walker A. (1989) 'Gender in Families: Women & Men in Marriage, Work & Parenthood *J of Marriage & The Family* 845

Trowell J. and Miles G. (1991) 'The Contribution of Observation Training to Professional Development in Social Work' *Journal of Social Work Practice* Vol. 5 No. 1

Tunnard J. (1991) 'Setting the Scene for Partnership' in (eds) Family Rights Group *The Children Act 1989: Working in Partnership with Families. Reader* 1 London: HMSO

Tunstill J. (26 Sept 1991) 'Not Yet a Bed of Roses' *Community Care. Inside* iv

Van Every J. (1991/2) 'Who is "the Family"? The Assumptions of British Social Policy' *Critical Social Policy* 62

Vogl R. (1991) *Initial Involvement* in Bala N., Hornick J. and Vogl R.N., (eds) *Canadian Child Welfare Law* Toronto: Thompson

Ward D. and Mullender A. (1990-2) *Critical Social Policy* 21-30

Warnock Report (1978) *Report of the Committee of Enquiry into the Education of Handicapped Children and Young People* London: HMSO

Waterhouse L. and Carnie J. (1992) 'Assessing Child Protection Risk' *Br. J Social Work* 47-60

Wattam C. (1992) *Making a Case in Child Protection* Harlow: NSPCC/Longman

Webb S.A. and McBeath G.B. (1989) 'A Political Critique of Kantian Ethics in Social Work' *British Journal of Social Work* 491

Whalley G. (1993) 'What is the Law of Education? Some Lessons from the Children Act 1989' *Education and the Law* 3-6

White R., Carr P. and Lowe N. (1990) *A Guide to the Children Act 1989* London: Butterworths

Whitney B. (1994) 'Letters to the Editor' *The Guardian* 18th June

Wildgoose J. (1987) 'Alternate Dispute Resolution in Child Protection Cases' *Canadian Journal of Family Law* 61

Williams J. (1992) 'Working Together II' *Journal of Child Law* 68

Wilson J. and Tomlinson M. (1986) *Wilson: Children and the Law* Toronto: Butterworths

Winnicott D.W. (1960) *The Theory of The Parent-Infant Relationship* in 'The Maturating Process and The Facilitating Environment' London: Hogarth

Winnicott D. W. (1964) *The Child, The Family and The Outside World* Harmondsworth: Penguin

Winnicott D. W. (1971) *Therapeutic Consultations in Child Psychiatry* London: Hogarth Press

Winnicott D. W. (1971) *Playing and Reality* Harmondsworth: Penguin

Winnicott D. W. (1977) *The Piggle* London: Hogarth Press

Winnicott D. W. (1979) *The Making and Breaking Of Affectional Bonds* London: Tavistock

Wolfendale S. (1988) *The Parental Contribution to Assessment* National Council for Special Education

Yard D. (1990) *Child and Family Services Legislation* Legal Studies Department, Law Society of Manitoba

The Contributors

Mark Berelowitz is Consultant Child and Adolescent Psychiatrist at the Royal Free Hospital in London. He has a special interest in child sexual abuse and has published in that field.

Alison Diduck is a lecturer in the Law Department at Brunel University and an Associate Director of the Centre for the Study of Law, the Child and the Family. She has taught and practised law in Manitoba, Canada, and now researches and teaches primarily in the fields of child and family law, and feminism and the law.

Felicity Kaganas is a lecturer in the Law Department at Brunel University where she is also an Associate Director of the Centre for the Study of Law, the Child and the Family. She has published in the UK and abroad on feminist issues and in the areas of child and family law.

Michael King is Professor Associate and Co-Director of the Centre for the Study of Law, the Child and the Family, Brunel University. He has published extensively in interdisciplinary fields involving law and the social sciences. He is at present engaged in developing and applying autopietic theory. His latest book, an edited volume, entitled *God's Law versus State Law: The Construction of an Islamic Identity in Western Europe*, will be published in 1995.

Brynna Kroll is a senior lecturer and post-graduate course leader in the Social Work Department at West London Institute of Brunel University where she specialists in probation practice, family work and direct work with children and adolescents. She is co-author of *The Probation Handbook* and author of *Chasing Rainbows: Children, Divorce and Loss*.

Judith Masson is Professor of Law at Warwick University and currently co-directing a Rowntree-funded project on *Partnership with 'Lost' Parents*. She advised *Voice for the Child in Care* on the Children Bill and subsequently worked with the Department of Health on the implementation programme for Part III of the Act.

Christine Piper is a lecturer in the Law Department at Brunel University where she is also Co-Director of the Centre for the Study of Law, the Child and the Family. Her recent publications include (with Michael King) *How the Law Thinks About Children* and *The Responsible Parent*.

Robin Solomon is a senior lecturer in the Social Work Department at the West London Institute of Brunel University where she specialises in child care, child development and therapeutic work with individuals. She is currently undertaking research in the field of social work at Hunter College, New York.

June Thoburn is a Professor of Social Work at the University of East Anglia and she is also a qualified social worker. She has researched and published widely on alternative placements for children in care, her most recent books being *Child Placement: Principles and Practice* and (with colleagues) *Paternalism or Partnership? The Involvement of Family Members in the Child Protection Process.*

Sarah Woodhouse is engaged in research for her doctorate examining the implementation of partnership under the Children Act 1989 in child protection work. She is based at the Centre for Socio-Legal Studies, Wolfson College, Oxford.

Subject Index

169

Author Index